Dialogue with a Difference

Dialogue with a Difference

The Manor House Group Experience

Edited by Tony Bayfield and Marcus Braybrooke

SCM PRESS LTD

ISBN 0 334 01980 X

First published 1992
by SCM Press Ltd
26–30 Tottenham Road
London N1 4BZ

Phototypeset by Intype, London
and printed in Great Britain by
Mackays of Chatham, Kent

Contents

The Manor House

Tony Bayfield

I wrote in my introduction to this book of a double inheritance, the Jewish tradition and the English culture which are both part of my birthright. By some strange twist of fortune, this dual birthright has pursued me in a particularly graphic way.

The Sternberg Centre for Judaism in Finchley, north-west London, is nothing other than the remaining seven-and-a-half acres of the ancient manor of Finchley. As the cover photograph illustrates, the present Manor House was built in 1723 but the manor of Finchley itself goes back to the time of King John. Indeed, one of the lords of the manor was executed at the Tower for an alleged affair with Anne Boleyn. Some years later the house burnt down, though traces of its moat still remain in the more impenetrable parts of our grounds. The Georgian house was acquired by the Sisters of Marie Auxiliatrice in 1918 who then engaged in an energetic building programme – adding a chapel, a school block and converting the old stables to form a convent and girls' school.

In 1981, this little corner of English history became surplus to the Order's requirements and was acquired by an independent group of Trustees and renamed the Manor House Centre for Judaism. It was soon to become the Sternberg Centre in recognition of the involvement of Sir Sigmund Sternberg, a Hungarian-born Jewish philanthropist, with particular interests in the field of Interfaith understanding.

The Sternberg Centre serves two interconnected functions. It is, first, the headquarters of non-Orthodox Judaism in Britain. As such, it is home to the Reform Synagogues of Great Britain, the umbrella organization for some forty Reform synagogues throughout the United Kingdom. The Centre also houses the Leo Baeck College, which trains rabbis, not only for Britain but for much of Europe and many other parts of the world. Akiva School, the first Progressive Jewish primary school, has taken over the convent school block and the nuns' chapel is now a synagogue.

The Centre also performs a function unique in Britain and perhaps unique in the rest of the world, certainly outside North America. It is a broadly-based, Jewish intellectual, educational and cultural centre, a place of meeting, outreach and interface. A list of organizations and programmes which emanate from the Sternberg Centre may give some clue as to its breadth and purpose. It contains a museum of Anglo-Jewish social history, a cultural society which mounts art exhibitions and musical recitals, a bookshop, a library and a cafeteria which is the base for an educational programme for young people with learning difficulties. It houses a Jewish educational agency which services the needs of synagogues and their Sunday schools; an organization reaching out to students at university; and a programme of training for the volunteer carers who visit the sick, comfort the bereaved and assist the elderly in Jewish communities nationwide. The Centre has a series of social clubs – for people in their twenties and for single, divorced and widowed people of all ages – and a 'chavurah' project which supports and promotes alternative, less formal modes of Jewish association. There are initiatives in the field of medical ethics, business ethics – and even a biblical garden. The Sternberg Centre publishes a quarterly journal, MANNA, which is a lively introduction to contemporary Jewish ideas and issues.

In the midst of all of this activity, interfaith work has always stood out. This book will tell its readers a great deal about the Manor House Dialogue Group. Its successor, a Jewish-Christian-Muslim Dialogue Group, is already taking shape.

One of the quiet revolutions in the Jewish world during the past twenty years has been the focus at Leo Baeck College on interfaith dialogue. In the new post-war Europe, with its multi-faith and multi-cultural environment, rabbinic studies can no longer be conducted in a ghetto – physical, intellectual or spiritual. The College has always included introductions to Christianity, Islam and eastern religions, taught where possible by representatives of the particular faith under discussion. It runs a biennial seminar at which some one hundred Christian theology students from all parts of the UK and abroad spend an intensive weekend studying at the College, living with Jewish families, attending services and sharing the life of the community.

Over the past twenty years the College has organized the annual Jewish-Christian-Muslim conference at the Hedwig Dransfeld Haus in Bendorf, Germany. Aimed at theology students of the three faiths, as well as social and community workers and teachers, it provides a unique forum for confronting the fears and prejudices that stand between the various faith communities, as well as exploring shared areas of agreement. It is one of the few forums for a shared debate on issues like the Middle East peace process, the Intifada, the Gulf War, the Salman Rushdie affair as they impact upon the communities here in Europe. That there now exists a network of rabbis and Christian and Muslim clergymen who see each other as colleagues and friends is a witness to the imagination, persistence and courage of all who have shared in this particular enterprise.

Akiva School also lays great stress on understanding the faith of other people within out multifaith society and its staff and children have developed warm relations with a number of churches, mosques and a Hindu temple.

As with many charitable institutions, so much is achieved with precarious and slender resources. Indeed, resources are a constant brake on the ideas and programmes which are well-nigh inexhaustible. But an open, outreaching, responsive centre of Jewish life must be a model worth nourishing and sustaining. For it renews and revitalizes an ancient tradition whilst allowing it to interact with many other traditions and with the distinctive post-Enlightenment English culture of the late twentieth century. In this way, the double inheritance is preserved and enriched and a truly pluralist society can develop to the benefit of all.

For further details, write to:
The Director,
The Sternberg Centre for Judaism,
The Manor House,
80 East End Road,
London N3 2SY

Foreword

STUART BLANCH

It could have been that my interest in Judaism arose from my experience of teaching the Old Testament in an Oxford theological college. But not so. The Oxford School of Theology required little knowledge of the so-called Intertestamental period and virtually none of the rabbinic Judaism which developed after the fall of Jerusalem in 70 CE. Or perhaps my interest in Judaism could have arisen from a series of visits to Israel. But I had only fleeting contacts with the Rainbow Group in Jerusalem, and the Kibbutz in which we sometimes stayed was secular in origin and practice. My first experience of Jewish-Christian dialogue was when I acted as joint-chairman with the Chief Rabbi in the first-ever official Anglican-Jewish consultation. It sticks in my memory for a remark made by a senior American rabbi who was present. 'We Jews,' he said, 'have no theology.'

I understand that remark better now, but it was distinctly startling for the Anglican delegates present. As a patient student of the Gospels, I could not be unaware of the fraught relationships between Jew and Christian reflected in them. But that was at a comfortable distance of 2000 years. So I was delighted and honoured to be invited to join the Manor House Group some seven years ago. I have contributed little to the group, but I have profited hugely from it, and I commend this book which has emerged unforced from our deliberations. Our discussions have never been less than friendly, but hallowed traditions on both sides of the fence have been subjected to careful, uncompromising scrutiny. It would have been a pity if the insights we have received had not been made available to the Jewish and Christian communities at large. I can only speak for the church and confess to the incomprehension which prevails on our side of the great divide. I have sometimes said that every church needs a notice over the door to the effect that 'Jesus was a Jew' – and perhaps that goes for the synagogue, too.

The American rabbi who startled the assembly with his assertion that the Jews had no theology no doubt intended to startle his Anglican

I

counterparts – and demonstrably did so. Nevertheless, no Christian biblical scholar could command a hearing if he did not take seriously the Jewish theological suppositions which underly the sacred text. And no Christian theologian could afford to ignore the effects of the dramatic separation of Christians from Judaism in the first century CE. Hellenism served well enough to provide the theologian with a language and a philosophy which helped to make Christianity accessible to the Western world. But a heavy price was paid for the almost total loss of the Jewish dimension and the hostility which was generated by the separation. Our dogmatic structures might have been less divisive in the church if more use had been made of our Jewish antecedents. But I hope that the kind of discussion in which we have been engaged in the group will not be confined to theologians and religious leaders.

Judaism has riches to dispense which civilization as a whole desperately needs. The Jewish people has lived out its life under diverse political and social conditions. It has survived the disappearance of seemingly invincible regimes. In this maelstrom of history Jewish thinkers have had cause to ponder and to comment on moral, political and social issues which have confronted them ever since Abraham left Ur for Canaan. In the process they have bequeathed to the modern world a whole range of literature, canonical and otherwise, incorporating law and custom, wisdom and ethics, philosophy and practice which is without rival in the history of our planet. In a civilization bedevilled by renascent nationalism, and a moral pluralism which borders on anarchy, we could do worse than resort to the riches of this Jewish tradition in its bearing on our 'modern' social and political dilemmas.

The questions we have been discussing in the group, with some disagreements but with a promising degree of coalescence, have recently been addressed by Professor Dunn.[1] He says: 'The crucial question to both Jew and Christian may be this: Can we let go our present sufficiently to recover our common past? And can we let go our separate past and present sufficiently to allow a common future to emerge from within the will of God in history?'[2] That is a crucial question for Jews and Christians, and of great significance also for the whole of the interfaith movement. I hope our book will encourage others to pursue it.

Introduction

I. TONY BAYFIELD

My dialogue with Christians has been a great blessing. Sometimes a mixed blessing, but a blessing nevertheless. For the last few years the Manor House Group has had a profound impact on me. It has got under my skin and infiltrated the deepest recesses of my mind. To explain how it all came about demands a brief biographical excursion.

I went up to Magdalene College, Cambridge, to read law in the autumn of 1965. My three years at Cambridge were extremely happy and I quickly found myself a firm circle of friends. One of our number was keen on rallying, which meant that he was allowed to keep a car in town – and that made him particularly popular. From time to time, we would commandeer both him and his car, and that was how I came to know the Essex/Suffolk border villages. My historian friends were considerably keener on visiting these exquisite monuments to the wool trade than they were on studying the written records that appeared so frequently on their reading lists. I wandered with them through Clare and into the great churches at Long Melford and Lavenham. I drank in both the aesthetics and the atmosphere.

Some years later, when I was studying for my rabbinic degree at the Leo Baeck College, I was to spend many hours with a brilliant Bible teacher called Ellen Littman. Dr Littman, the name by which she was always known, was a German Jewish refugee. When I looked unimpressed as she was extolling the virtues of Buber's translation of the Hebrew Bible into German, she would say to me, 'Mr Bailey (she never could get my name right), you are so English.' Had I responded, 'Dr Littman, you are so German', she would have been profoundly hurt. So much of Jewish history is encapsulated in that interchange, and I am aware of the foolishness that can be imputed to my love and nostalgia for all those villages and churches which are so quintessentially English. Indeed, there are few things more foolish than unrequited love. But love seldom comes at any person's bidding.

I went from Cambridge to rabbinic training college and thence to my

3

first congregational assignment in Weybridge, Surrey. I spent more than a decade there, but the focus of my work was the building up of a Jewish congregation. I made little time for contacts outside the Jewish community. I should qualify that by saying that, during the course of my years in north-west Surrey, I gave countless talks to innumerable non-Jewish groups. I spoke in schools, to societies of many kinds, and to a considerable number of church groups, and even preached in one or two churches. But this was giving information on Judaism and public relations work, with little element of real dialogue.

During this period, questions began to form, but I found few people with whom to discuss them. On days off my wife and I would try to go out – if only to get away from the 'phone – and trips out would sometimes include a visit to a beautiful church or a magnificent cathedral. An ambiguity began to clarify itself. This was part of my English inheritance and I responded to it. But I am the heir to a double inheritance, and as a Jew I was often ill at ease. I was an outsider here. What readings from the Gospels still slandered my ancestors, the Scribes and Pharisees? What words had been preached about Jews from this pulpit? What attitude would the clergy here adopt to me, a Jew, and to my faith?

Towards the end of my time in Weybridge, we took a cottage in Northumberland for a fortnight's summer holiday. The cottage was at Alnmouth, which I remember for its wonderful expanse of sand, a beach which we had entirely to ourselves and our anoraks. More significantly, I remember that holiday for a particular piece of serendipity.

I was not a particularly generous father and insisted as soon as I decently could that my children must have had enough of the kind of things that children actually enjoy doing on holiday and, instead, that we should go for drives and explore. Much to my children's disgust, one drive took us to yet another old ruin (they insist it was always either old ruins or National Trust houses!) – the ruins of Brinkburn Priory beside the River Coquet. From my point of view it was the most perfect spot – the most beautiful, austere shell, a flowing river and utter peace. My wife took the children down to the river to have a picnic and I wandered back into the church. As I stood there the prayers that had been prayed in that place became tangible. I was overwhelmed with the conviction that those prayers were good prayers, true prayers, laid before the same Ultimate Reality addressed by prayers in the synagogue.

Thinking both of Brinkburn and Long Melford I was later to try to explain my feelings to a residential conference of the Council of Christians and Jews in Suffolk:

I look up to the roof soaring above me heavenwards. And around at the empty pews. The prayers prayed in this place for centuries are almost tangible. Real prayers, honest prayers, true prayers, prayers which are heard. People reach out to God here, just as I strive to reach out to God in synagogue. And if they reach out to God, God comes to meet them here. The smell, the flavour, the accoutrements may not be of my home, but God is as at home here as God is at my house.[1]

In 1983 I moved from Weybridge to become Director of the Sternberg Centre for Judaism in Finchley, north-west London. By now, a particular issue was becoming clearer. I was and still am aware of antisemitism. Ignorance and prejudice are too widespread and too dangerous to ignore, and one should never underestimate the anxiety that they provoke, quite justifiably, in the Jewish community. But antisemitism is far from being central to the focus of my life and does not define either my identity or my faith.

Years of explaining Judaism, Jewish practice and Jews to a vast array of groups have been an important part of my work. But once again it is not the core. More important, I have (I hope) long since escaped the trap of feeling the need to justify my Judaism, to have it defined by other people's faith and beliefs, to present it in a way that distorts in order to ingratiate. Although a liberal, I am as passionately committed to my faith, tradition and people as any more separatist and visually distinctive exponent of Judaism.

But in the course of my career and life I have encountered a number of Christians (and Muslims) whose life and faith have so impressed me that a conviction has been brought home to me with ever-growing strength. That conviction has to do with the integrity of their place of worship, with the validity of their prayers, with the acceptability to God of their faith. If that intuitive understanding has any importance (and I believe it has), then it is necessary for me to formulate my own self-understanding and theology as a Jew in a way that leaves space – uncondescending, unequivocal space – for my Christian (and Muslim) friends. This is a space which (I should add lest there be any confusion) does not compromise in any way the integrity of my own Jewish faith and commitment. How to do it? How to make space? How to talk about Christianity? How to express the existential insight in coherent theology?

Just before I became Director of the Sternberg Centre, I met Marcus Braybrooke, soon to become Executive Director of the Council of Christians and Jews. I recognized almost instantly that Marcus was going to be special to me. His faith left space for Jews, and he too was grappling with a theology which would be consonant with his intuitive understanding. I felt that Marcus was someone I could work with, and it came as no surprise

5

to me when he supplied the explanation for our rapport. He, too, was a graduate of Magdalene College, Cambridge!

I will shortly hand this introduction on to Marcus to fill in the details and describe the establishment of the Manor House Group. Before I do so I would like to offer a few brief observations.

I am desperate to avoid maudlin platitudes about a dialogue group having 'changed my life'. But I must, nevertheless, be honest and say that I have discovered certain very important things in the context of this particular dialogue.

First, people of faith in the closing years of the twentieth century can have a great deal in common. On many issues that we struggled with in the group, disagreements and nuances did not fall along party lines. I discovered that a number of my Christian colleagues were struggling with exactly the same issues as I was, whilst others had resolved problems for themselves, just as some of my Jewish colleagues had resolved them.

Second, the group bore out for me the importance of trust. Continuity of membership ensured the development of familiarity and friendship. And from friendship sprang trust. Last year I edited a progressive Jewish 'platform', a statement of what liberal Jews like me believe. I realized that a significant part of the exploration and clarification of my own beliefs had actually been done in dialogue. Dialogue has not shaken my Jewish faith, but it has enriched it and developed it in many subtle ways. Dialogue has proved to be a setting with great potential for personal religious growth and clarification.

Third, I discovered just how inhibiting the politics of religion can be. So much gets filtered, censored and removed from the public domain by the fears and constraints that come with office. I hope that my own contribution to this book has not been too significantly inhibited by excessive fear of the likely 'political' consequences. John Bowden draws a sharp distinction between ideology and truth, and I have come to understand that both Jews and Christians all too easily fail to notice the distinction.

In planning this book, we decided that the best way of translating discussion into writing was for four members of the group to make extended statements in four areas – the areas that the Group had spent most time discussing. Other members of the Group would then respond to each of these core essays – two respondents to each statement. Norman Solomon would endeavour to summarize the process. We are very conscious of not having been able to deal with each of the chosen topics more fully. Furthermore, many challenging and important areas have not been touched on at all. The absence of a section on Israel, for instance, is significant. It was probably the area where least was moved forward and most discomfort was experienced, although two helpful papers have been published.[2] This is sad, because I remember saying at a very early meeting that I came as a 'package'. If in dialogue we seek acceptance at some level, then it is not enough to accept Tony Bayfield, lover of Essex/Suffolk border villages, since Tony Bayfield, Zionist, is inseparable from his other persona.

Unrequited love is enormously painful. The Christian contributors to this book are by no means representative of all Christians. The corollary to the space which I wish to give to Christianity is equal space for Judaism – space unsullied by supersessionism, contempt or missionary intent. For some, for many, that reciprocity may not be on offer. Which leaves me sad, angry and feeling rather foolish by turns. But the loving, caring response of many within the group and this book is sufficient encouragement. And who ever suggested that perceptions of truth come only with joy and never with pain?

II. MARCUS BRAYBROOKE

No one told me that the Manor House, East Finchley, was nowhere near Manor House tube station. It was a long hot walk before I arrived, a little late. Even when I discovered nearer stations, the Northern Line usually conspired to make me late.

My first visit to Manor House was before I had been appointed as Executive Director of the Council of Christians and Jews.[1] Together with the Roman Catholic Bishop Konstant, I had been asked, at short notice, to speak to a meeting of Reform rabbis. I forget what I said, but I came away with a clear impression that the rabbis wanted more than just the 'tea and biscuits' talk which followed a tour of a synagogue. They showed their anger and pain at the churches' continuing missionary efforts, at Christians' insensitivity to Israel and at surviving anti-Jewish teaching and attitudes. They wanted to talk in depth about these matters with some Christians, not merely show off the synagogue to admiring groups.

A television appearance by Tony led me to correspond with him. Then, late in 1983, some of the Reform rabbis came from their annual conference at Ammerdown near Bath to be received at the Palace in Wells by the then bishop, John Bickersteth, and to tour the cathedral. Bishop Bickersteth encouraged me to contact some Christian leaders, especially Stuart Blanch, to see whether a small informal Jewish-Christian dialogue group could be established.

I met with Tony, who was now Director of the Manor House – yet to be renamed the Sternberg Centre – late in 1983. We both felt that a 'small, coherent ongoing group in which people could encounter each other in depth was desirable'.[2] There were already a number of lectures arranged by Jewish-Christian societies, followed by public discussion. The Rainbow Group regularly had papers from distinguished speakers but its membership had become diffuse, so that there was not much continuity of discussion from one meeting to the next. We agreed that it was important that in the new group those who joined should make attendance a high

8

priority. This allowed for continuity and the development of trust, as Tony has already pointed out. It meant that some initial members found that other commitments made it impossible for them to continue. It also proved difficult to integrate those who joined the group more recently – partly because dates had already been fixed. Yet the regularity of attendance of a core group has given continuity and meant that I certainly look forward to meetings as a chance to be with friends. This commitment and continuity – demanding as it is – is an important factor in a interfaith group which wants to explore issues in some depth.

It was decided deliberately to limit membership to those who shared assumptions about the value of dialogue and critical thought. This did not mean that the group was monochrome, and we quickly found that Christians disagreed with Christians and Jews with Jews, but it implied some shared assumptions. Most of the Jews, except for Norman Solomon and Jeremy Rosen, were Reform or Liberal Jews, and all the Christians were Anglicans, except for Sister Margaret Shepherd, who was initially the scribe (though after a time she decided either that we said too much or that our words were not worth recording verbatim!). The self-limitation of membership meant that we engaged more quickly with deeper issues. The choice of members for a group relates closely to its purpose – and too often in dialogue situations neither the aims nor the assumptions are clearly enough defined, so that some people feel uneasy. In our case, John Goldingay, who played a significant part in our early meetings, eventually found that the dominant critical assumptions of the most vocal members marginalized his contribution.

From the beginning, it was made clear that the group was unofficial, and members were in no way 'representatives' – although the meetings were generously hosted by the Sternberg Centre. Even so, as some of the group became better known in public life, public controversies, especially the 'Forgiveness Debate', which was sparked off by articles in *The Times* by Albert Friedlander and Anthony Phillips, then Chaplain at St John's College, Oxford, affected the life of the group.[3] We were all saddened when Anthony, because of new work, withdrew from the group.

Initially we hoped that the group would have a life of two years. That it has lasted for nearly eight shows its vitality, and the meeting following our decision to disband was one of the most lively. We felt, however, that because of inevitable changes of membership it was difficult to ensure continuing momentum. It may also be that the time has come to form new groups. It is certainly clear that we have not reached agreement on the key issues that we have discussed – perhaps we merely see more clearly how complex they are. This is why this book tries to reflect something of the dynamism of dialogue, and we hope that it encourages readers to join in the conversation.

Tony's and my suggestion was that we should meet twice a year for a whole day and once a year for a two-day residential gathering – for which Charney Manor in Oxfordshire became a regular home.

Charney Manor, a Friends' Conference Centre, is an old manor house set in the Oxfordshire countryside. The little church next door has the characteristic scent of English sanctity, which Tony has mentioned.

The residential time allowed us to relax and to let personal friendships grow. Richard Harries' guided ramble through part of his diocese became a regular feature and most of the urban rabbis found it wise to invest in a pair of boots – although some escaped to Blackwells.

These times together led us in a hesitant way to ask about our life of prayer. One presumed that each of us did our 'own thing' in our rooms. Should there, in addition, be some corporate prayer or, at least, might we say grace at mealtimes? Quaker silence was the easiest option. Particular patterns of daily prayer are part of the traditional life of a faith community. Prayer together is not a substitute for these, but some of us felt an important dimension of our sharing was missing if we could not be together in the acknowledged presence of God. Presumably if we had been at a clergy or rabbinical conference corporate prayer would have been *de rigueur*. Eventually we introduced a time of shared meditation and reflection, which some found helpful. There was, however, no hesitancy about shared sessions of Bible study which were always vigorous and stimulating.[4]

To return to the planning: it may be interesting to look at the original agenda which Tony and I suggested.

(*a*) Is there a respectable philosophical and religious basis to pluralism? What do we mean by the image of the prism in which God is the light on one side and Judaism and Christianity see the same light refracted in different colours? What does this do to concepts such as Christian uniqueness and Jewish chosenness? Are there real depths to our tolerance and liberalism?

(i) In the light of the above, how do we look at Paul and the New Testament? Can we understand and teach the New Testament in a way which neither belittles nor causes offence?

(ii) In the light of the above, how do we view Israel, and what may each expect of the other in this regard?

(*b*) Given the evil of the twentieth century, how does each faith affirm a God of love and how is its view of the other affected by the terms of that affirmation?[5]

The deliberate decision to discuss 'theological' issues has been significant. At the time, the Council of Christians and Jews, out of deference to Orthodox Jews, avoided 'theological' issues and out of deference to some Christians it avoided questions about 'mission'. Lest it appeared 'political', it did not discuss Israel either. Under Lord Coggan's leadership, in the 1980s, CCJ rejected this quiet life as the kiss of death.[6] Through my work for CCJ, I was able to share more widely some of the issues being discussed at the Manor House Group.

For some Christians, the interest in dialogue was – and still is – essentially self-centred. It may be a wish to learn more about the historical setting of Jesus and his roots in Judaism. It may be prompted by guilt about the Shoah (or Holocaust).[7] This may inspire heroic efforts to purge Christianity of its age-old anti-Judaism, but the guilt may hinder meeting the other as other. For some Jews, an interest in dialogue was to make Christians aware of and get rid of their anti-Judaism. For others – sometimes exploiting the 'guilt' – it was to win sympathy for the state of Israel. Yet dialogue which has an agenda other than seeking the 'truth' is essentially ideological: it has a further motivation outside the dialogue itself. Genuine dialogue may be content with building up trust and friendship or encouraging common action for social good – as Norman indicates (p. 161). Yet at its deepest, dialogue allows the partners to share their convictions and confront their differences. In this way, in the words of the American Reform theologian Eugene Borowitz, 'It shows its conviction that truth is ultimately one'.[8]

The aim of dialogue is not to suggest that all religions say the same thing, nor just to uphold the other's right to be wrong. It springs from the deep conviction of God's activity in the whole of human history and of God's presence within the various religious traditions of humankind. It implies that whatever has been believed is worthy of serious consideration. As Christian theology is now a joint endeavour of Anglicans, Catholics and Protestants, so interfaith dialogue points towards the possibility of global theology. Certainly Christian theology is being enriched as it begins to share the Jewish inheritance.

This process does not empty commitment of meaning, but challenges it in open discussion. Our convictions are tested in free debate, without the protection of scriptural or ecclesiastical authority. It can be a searing process, but most who have shared deeply in dialogue affirm that their central convictions have been strengthened, whilst at the same time they have been purified and enriched by a newly discovered reverence for the faith of others and respect for those who hold such faith.

One of the blessings of dialogue is that it may be a means of growth. It is not just a matter of understanding the other – important as this is. If one listens attentively, one begins to ask questions and reconsider one's own beliefs. This is a life process – not religious 'negotiation' nor an attempt to find some accommodating compromise. Rather, dialogue is a spur to one's own theological rethinking.[9] Too few in the churches as yet seem ready for this theological rethinking. I hope this book may encourage others to recognize that the blessings of such exploration outweigh the risks.

The commitment and openness which are characteristic of dialogue at its best are necessary if people of faith are not only to overcome past misunderstanding and prejudice but also to work together for a just and peaceful world. Dialogue is not just a blessing to the individual participant, but may be a blessing to us all if, in Norman Solomon's words, it plays a part in 'the heroic drama of saving humankind from self-destruction' (p. 162).

Part One
Making Theological Space for Each Other

1. Making Theological Space

TONY BAYFIELD

All too often Jewish-Christian conversations fail to move beyond the ideological – the pressing of a particular agenda, the 'brokering of deals', or the justification of slogans. But there can come a point in the dialogue when the attempt to gain ideological advantage gives way to the quest for understanding and truth.[1] At that point, the dialogue becomes powerful and potentially iconoclastic. Faith is exposed in all its vulnerability, and the questions asked of it will be unique. For the questions will not be those of co-religionists with shared assumptions, of intra-faith rivals or of secularists – the usual trinity of Jewish conversationalists. Instead, the conversation is with those from a different, but uniquely and inextricably related, faith tradition. The result is new insight, change and fresh understanding. In listening to the language of others, one comes to hear one's own words in a new way. In trying to share not the public language of ideology but the private languages of faith,[2] both will grow. And a central question should inevitably press in upon each participant. What place do I give to these people in my map of faith? How do I acknowledge their country and how do I regard it?

The need to redraw the theological map

In the conclusion to his *Contemporary Christologies. A Jewish Response*, Eugene Borowitz, the greatest living liberal Jewish theologian, says of Christians with whom he had been in dialogue:

> I remain very much moved by the spirit of the men and women I have been exposed to here. For all that I differ with them and have, at given points, been roused to indignation by their ideas, I know myself to have been in the presence of believers, some of the profundity of whose faith I could palpably feel and share. In their struggles to sense and articulate their Christian belief I have seen something of what I and others

concerned with thinking rigorously about Judaism have been going through. In their effort to be realistic about personal and social existence, while being true to what God wants and Christian belief demands of them today, I have been touched by their courage and wisdom. For me this has been a most uncommon intellectual experience because it has been so existentially moving. I deem it appropriate, therefore, to give thanks to God who has given me this privilege.[3]

Dialogue, at least from the transformative point that I have indicated onwards, is not just an intellectual and political experience but an emotional and spiritual one as well. Borowitz is right to offer thanks, but there are insistent questions which follow from the dialogue experience that demand a rigorous response. How am I to regard the religion of these people who have so challenged and moved me? What am I to say about their beliefs? How do I accommodate the palpable reality of their faith into my own theological map?

The questions first coalesced for me in a simple image. One of my early dialogue partners was an Anglican minister, vicar of my local parish church. One Saturday morning, I came out of my front door to set off for synagogue. I looked up the road to see my friend who had just emerged from *his* home, and was about to unlock his church. 'What does God make of all this?', I mused. Would God want him to throw away the keys and join me on the journey to synagogue? Or would God prefer me to change my Sabbath and my route to worship?

On reiterating the question, I have been told that it is impertinent and illegitimate to try to scrutinize the mind of God. Leaving aside my suspicion that trying to understand what God wants of us has played a considerable part in both Jewish and Christian thought, it seems to me that while I may have posed the question in a facile and impertinent manner, it is nevertheless a wholly/holy pertinent question to pose.

I have the distinct impression that certain consistent presuppositions underlie the warm and positive smiles of many of the most sincere dialoguers. 'You Jews really are remarkable for your persistence, contribution to civilization, family life and chicken soup. And, of course, we can learn so much from you about the roots of our faith and the community in which Jesus lived. But you are missing out on the greatest truth of all, which is a pity for you.' 'You Christians really have captured the lion's share of the market in spectacular fashion; your cathedrals are magnificent and you really are outstanding exponents of self-sacrificing, suffering love for the poor and sick. But it is all founded on a complete misunderstanding of the nature of a relatively unremarkable Jew and it is quite hard to know how you can still believe some of that stuff about incarnation.'

When dialogue moves to the point where real faith is exposed and engages, the presuppositions will not do. They are condescending, blocking and, above all, wholly inadequate in their treatment of people clearly moved by God and driven by faith. The existential reality demands a change in the theology which describes and explains that reality. To be useful, theology has to accommodate the independent integrity of two faiths, clearly truthful and sustaining, either of which only a vandal would wish to obliterate. God (who, of course, speaks Yiddish!) says both to me and my neighbour, *'Gey gesundaheit'*, 'Go in my service in peace'. And if that is so, what follows?

The 'warrant' for redrawing the map

Honest liberals should not need a warrant from tradition to believe everything that they believe. Furthermore, Jewish tradition, encompassing nearly four millennia of lives in diverse countries the world over, can readily be used selectively to 'prove' or 'disprove' most things. Above all, the past with its different mind-set and agenda should not be manipulated dishonestly to suit contemporary needs. What citations from tradition can offer are fingerprints, clues to the idiosyncratic personality of a particular inheritance and insight into why we are as we are.

I believe that Rosemary Ruether, a radical American theologian, is substantially correct when she says:

> Views of other nations, or 'gentiles', have varied in Jewish tradition from an ethnocentric hostility that sees the other nations as evil ones that will be defeated and destroyed by God, to a benign liberalism that seeks a *modus vivendi* among all peoples through common standards of humanitarianism, thus leaving Jews to pursue their own distinctive religious and cultural path.[4]

Reversing the order of Ruether's comments, there are already indications within the Hebrew Bible of an ability implicit in Judaism to acknowledge and respect the religious territory of others. One thinks immediately of the Book of Jonah, in which Jonah, the Jewish prophet, goes to Nineveh to call upon the inhabitants to repent. They do so and are forgiven by God. Although Jonah himself appears angered and confused by the turn of events and seems never to grasp the true purpose of his mission, the author is content to affirm an effective process of prayer, repentance and forgiveness independent of Jews and Judaism. God is the God of the whole world, and the nations of the world have access to God in their own way.[5] Malachi would appear to make a similar point quite succinctly: 'For from where the sun rises to where it sets, my name is honoured amongst the nations, and everywhere incense and pure oblation are offered to my name; for my name is honoured amongst the nations – says the Lord of Hosts.'[6] When Micah writes: 'For let all the peoples walk each one in the name of its god, but we will walk in the name of the Lord our God for ever',[7] we are left with a nuance which may be characteristic. The acknowledgment of the faith of others is clear, as is a preparedness to leave them to their own devices. However, there is a suspicion of value judgment which I have tried to bring out in the capitalizing of Micah's God, but not the god of 'all the peoples'.

Judaism was and is a love affair with God – the image is in itself biblical, as witness Hosea's famous betrothal statement: 'I betroth you to me for ever, I betroth you to me with integrity and justice, with tenderness and love. I betroth you to me with faithfulness and you will know the Lord.'[8] Like all great romances, the Jewish love affair has a tendency to be self-centred and contains the seeds of introversion. One could cite many biblical texts to support the latter assertion. But there are clearly many biblical authors who do not deny the possibility that others too may love and be loved by God.[9]

Early rabbinic Judaism was much concerned with the evil of worshipping idols and contains many passages attacking idolatry. Ruether may have had these in mind, as well as biblical passages about the conquest of Canaan, when she referred to 'ethnocentric hostility'. Yet even in this context there are more open sentiments. A Talmudic statement dating from the first two centuries of the Common Era declares: 'Our Rabbis taught, "On seeing the sages of Israel one should say, 'Blessed be he who has bestowed a portion of his wisdom on them that fear Him.' On seeing the sages of the idolators, one should say, 'Blessed be he who has given of his wisdom to his creatures.' " '[10] A rabbinic debate from the same period ends in the acceptance of the view of Rabbi Joshua that the righteous of all the nations of the world have a share in the world to come.[11] This view found further expression in the much-quoted: 'I call heaven and earth to witness that whether it be Jew or gentile, man or woman, manservant or maidservant, only according to their deeds does the Holy Spirit rest upon them.'[12]

The earliest history of Jewish-Christian relations is full of tension and acrimony. Almost to our own day, these hostilities have continued, though the balance of power quickly reversed. Similarly, Jewish-Islamic relations, though usually less violent, were scarcely a model of mutually accepting tolerance.[13] Nevertheless, at the height of the Middle Ages, when oppression of Judaism by Christianity and Islam was at its zenith, Judaism acknowledged that Islam was not idolatry, about gods, but a form of monotheism, about God.[14]

Gradually Jews, notably the great French Jewish Bible commentator, Rashi (1040–1105), extended the same perception to Christianity, even though the Trinity presented particular problems to mediaeval Jewish theologians concerned to uphold the purity of monotheism.[15] The Spanish Jewish philosopher, Bahya ibn Pakuda (late eleventh century), relied extensively on Sufi scholars and vigorously defended his right to use gentiles as teachers of religion, referring to them as 'saints', *chasidim*.[16] Even the greatest Jewish thinker of the Middle Ages, Maimonides (Spain, 1135–1204), whose jaundiced view of Christianity and Islam was rooted in personal experience of both the sword and the scimitar, says: 'All these events (relating to Jesus) and even those relating to him who succeeded the one referred to (Muhammad), were nothing else than a means for preparing the way for the King Messiah. It will reform the whole world to worship God with one accord . . .'[17]

In the eighteenth century, the scholar Jacob Emden (1707–1776) wrote:

The founder of Christianity conferred a double blessing upon the world: on the one hand he strengthened the Torah of Moses, and emphasized its eternal obligatoriness. On the other hand he conferred favour upon the heathen in removing idolatry from them, imposing upon them stricter moral obligations than are contained in the Torah of Moses. There are many Christians of high qualities and excellent morals. Would that all Christians would live in conformity with their precepts! They are not enjoined, like the Israelites, to observe the laws of Moses, nor do they sin if they associate other beings with God in worshipping a triune God. They will receive a reward from God for having propagated a belief in Him among nations that never heard His name: for He looks into the heart.[18]

The purpose of a survey of the past

If this recitation of selected quotations is meant neither to be a warrant nor a self-justification, what is its purpose? Its purpose is two-fold. First, to suggest that the Jewish covenant, sense of chosenness, mission, love affair with God has usually left scope to acknowledge the possibility of meaningful religious lives beyond the Jewish world. But, as Rosemary Ruether so perceptively suggests: 'The affirmation of Jewish distinctiveness left room for other peoples to affirm their own distinctiveness as well, *although it is not clear whether the distinctiveness of the others is really on the same level before God as that of the one "chosen" people.*'[19] It is precisely that issue of 'same level before God' which needs addressing and will form a focus of the latter part of this chapter.

Second, Judaism, lived as a community love affair with God, has sometimes bred an indifference to the spiritual life of others. It is a risk inherent in the passion. Nevertheless, this is scarcely the dominant factor accounting for the not inconsiderable amount of hostility and suspicion of the non-Jewish world which has existed within many Jewish communities through the centuries. Much of this is a response to external attitudes and behaviour. 'Surrounded by a succession of imperialistic peoples – the Hellenistic, Greco-Roman, Islamic and Christian empires, each of which had claimed to have the key to the one true humanity and the one authentic relationship to the Divine . . .',[20] confronted by such triumphal imperialism, Jews often turned in on themselves and regarded those outside the group with a considerable weight of negative feelings. Borowitz cites the Talmudic blessing for non-Jewish scholars quoted earlier.[21] He then details the gradual whittling away of its sphere of operation as the Middle Ages progressed. There can be little doubt that this seeping away of generosity was a reaction to external circumstances. An imperialistic belief in a monopoly on truth and a determination to thrust it down the throats of others is not conducive to trust and openness. Jewish introversion and Christian imperialism are both understandable in terms of world history and the history of ideas. But they have left their mark and are still to be found in the presuppositions which I described earlier as lying behind the smiles round the dialogue table. The reality of each other's faith demands that, after two thousand years, we try to move on.

The barrier of contempt

I suggested in my paragraph on presuppositions that Jews tend to regard Christianity as founded upon a mistake, though they are often too polite to say so. The mistake is about reading theologically into the life of Jesus not only that which is unwarranted but also that which runs counter to fundamental Jewish ideas about the nature of God. Christ incarnate would appear to present an immense block to an acknowledgment which has any worth to it.

The block is, let me reiterate, more than merely textual or doctrinal. The history of the last millennium has left a deep well of Jewish anger which will not be resolved overnight. There is a chain of suspicion which begins with 'do you still seek to convert me?' and runs through the continued association of some leaders of the Church of England with organizations devoted to mission to the Jews[22] back to the forced conversions and massacres of the Middle Ages. That the Christian participants acknowledge

Judaism as of independent salvific value and that they are prepared to acknowledge that Jews can be left to be Jews is not a prerequisite for dialogue. Yet without such explicit acknowledgment it is exceedingly difficult for the dialogue to move beyond the pragmatic and ideological. Furthermore, until such acknowledgment is clear, many Jews are reluctant to make concessions on the 'founded on a mistake' presupposition. Indeed, any Jew who does what I wish to do and challenges that presupposition is likely to experience some of the displaced anger that properly belongs with more than a millennium of contempt and denial.

The core affirmation

But the risk has to be taken, and Jewish-Christian relations must ultimately be founded on theological truth rather than ideological negotiations.[23] What is it, then, that I feel compelled to say? It is this. I believe that many Christians find in the life and death of Jesus as described in the New Testament and in the tradition which flows from those events the fullest disclosure of the nature of God and God's will for them. Such faith involves no necessary error or illusion. I feel both comfortable with that affirmation and compelled to make it. However, we need to explore further its religious and intellectual basis and implications.

The barrier of scripture

In his recent book *Divine Action* Keith Ward, now Regius Professor at Oxford, has some interesting things to say about the Hebrew Bible. He suggests:

> The narratives seek to bring out the spiritual meaning of events which are far in the past, and have been recalled through long oral traditions and re-enacted in generations of ritual celebrations. They thus reflect the sorts of relations to God which the community of the final writers and editors felt themselves to have, inextricably intertwined and projected back onto memories of far distant events which have been treasured as founding-events of the Israelite community . . . The final account will be a sort of superposition of spiritual symbols upon an irrecoverable core of historical memory . . . The forms . . . and the symbols . . . are many-layered conceptual frameworks of spiritual meaning, which reflect the culture and interests of those to whom that revelation came.[24]

Much of what Ward has to say is equally applicable to the New

Testament. Of course, the gap between the events portrayed and the writing up of them is far shorter, but the same processes are at work and the literature is of a similar kind. With that premise in mind, I can accept the New Testament as a document out of which God speaks to Christians.

Clearly this is to acknowledge the New Testament as a book of revelation. In so doing, I am very aware of the considerable volume of anti-Judaism contained within the text. I would emphasize the gap between the disclosure events and their articulation in words and symbols; between the historical context and the reworking of historical events for theological purposes. But that God is present in those events, words and symbols whatever the complexities and flaws of transmission, redaction, interpretation and doctrine is clear.

The process of trying to lay bare the historical reality behind the texts of either of our Bibles is a stimulating and thought-provoking enterprise. Indeed it has done much to identify the significant element of Christian-Jewish polemic in the New Testament, which not only has to be recognized but dealt with if Christian-Jewish relations are to develop along more harmonious lines. But I do not feel that it is in any way to dismiss or undervalue such historical work to suggest that contemporary Judaism and Christianity share a strong tendency to overload the historical.

History is, according to Arthur A. Cohen, the American Jewish theologian, the domain of human freedom.[25] However, the point at which God and history meet can only be grasped and described in the form of myth. To treat that myth as if it were only history is to overload the historical. Conversely, to treat the meeting as if it were wholly extra-historical is to shackle humanity to its own limited historical and mythical vision.

There are moments in human history when the veil between God and humanity is parted and, through the chink, light flows. Sinai and Calvary represent such disclosure events. From that point on, light flows continually as through part-drawn curtains. If one moves to the window, one gets no closer to the source of light. The metaphor is an imperfect one, but I share with John Bowden[26] a suspicion that it is not just in the Hebrew Bible that the past is in some senses irrecoverable, and much historical scrutiny of the moments at which the veil was parted represents a forlorn pursuit of the Unprovable rather than a journeying with It into the future. God touches and is present in history but, like the genius of a painting, is seldom best discerned by subjecting the composition to historical analysis alone. However, if we understand the true nature of the literature and its purpose, we can discern behind the complex surface of history, symbol, redaction, interpretation and doctrine the sure signs that God has passed this way.

A pain and a puzzle to Jews

At this point, some Jews may well respond by interjecting: if God *intended* the revelation at Calvary as a complementary revelation to that at Sinai, then why should God have wished upon us all of the suffering which flowed from that act? Christianity may have been 'good for the world' but it certainly has not always been 'good for the Jews'!

There is a curious and challenging passage in an essay by the critic George Steiner. Wrestling with the problem of theodicy and the suffering of the Jews in the twentieth century, their apparent abandonment by God, Steiner writes:

> God suffers gusts of murderous exasperation at the Jews, towards a people who have made Him a responsible party to history and to the grit of man's condition. He may not have wished to be involved; *the people may have chosen Him, in the oasis at Kadesh, and thrust upon Him the labour of justice and right anger. It may have been the Jews who caught Him by the skirt, insisting on contact and dialogue.* Perhaps before either God or living man was ready for proximity.[27]

I am not sure that I find Steiner's observations helpful in terms of theodicy, but the picture of human beings as it were forcing the revelatory end, seizing the hem of God's skirt, tearing a hole in the curtain, is helpful. If we, in part, force the moments, then the question as to why God should choose this time and this place with all its historical consequences becomes less puzzling and less urgent.

No uncritical acceptance

God speaks to many through the events, words and symbols of the New Testament. That does not mean that I, as a Jew, do not have a host of questions about specific doctrines that have been erected upon that text (and, indeed, about the text itself). In dialogue, I can come to understand better what Christians mean.[28] Significantly, I discover that Christians mean many different things. Borowitz's analysis of various contemporary christologies is a case in point.[29] There is always room for indicating that certain perspectives are more congenial than others or for saying 'I do not understand'. And there is always room for saying 'I find that particular teaching contrary to my understanding of the nature of God' or simply unethical. But what I also continually find is that many of the ideas and insights are ones which Judaism has explored through different (though related) texts, myths and metaphors. After all, our histories are inextricably interwoven and our landscapes touch and overlap at countless points.[30] That is not to say that Judaism and Christianity are ultimately 'the same' (whatever that might mean). It is to assert that we each have texts in which disclosure events are trapped in an amalgam of history, symbol, interpretation and doctrine. That in our desperate search for certainty and fidelity we can each overload the historical and misunderstand the symbolic and mythical. But, above all, it is to insist that I find my Christian partners dedicated to the realization of a familiar goodness and prompted by a revealing metaphysical Reality which points to a coincidence of ultimate truths.[31]

To the last sticking point: the best, the truest

Dialogue is almost always possible and usually worthwhile. Even a member of The Church's Ministry to the Jewish People and a Lubavitch *chasid* could have a useful conversation. Deeper understanding is a perpetual possibility and, in a world where there are still a host of 'political' issues between Jews and Christians, worthwhile deals can be struck.

However, dialogue will be far richer if the parties can reach the point we have reached so far – acknowledging the worth of the two independent faiths and permitting their exponents to be themselves.

But there is still a presupposition to be dealt with. Many of the people sitting round the dialogue table still hold to a belief that their religion is best – better, truer – at a higher level than the religion of their partner.[32] This carries the inevitable implication that, if my religion is better, truer and higher than yours, I have an obligation not merely to share my 'good news' but also to point out to you the deficiencies of your faith and guide you towards my higher truth. Before my map is complete, it is that triumphalist and competitive thinking that I want to challenge.

The issue is most frequently articulated these days in the context of the debate on pluralism. The last few years have seen a spate of attacks on the pluralist position in general and on the thinking of its best known Protestant exponent, John Hick, in particular. This chapter is not a defence of pluralism, still less a discussion of all religions. It is solely concerned with the relationship between Judaism and Christianity. Nevertheless, some of the criticism directed at Hick seems rooted in the triumphalism and competitiveness which has been so damaging to Christian-Jewish relations over the centuries.

Is Judaism better or truer than Christianity or vice versa? I have more than a suspicion that the question itself is largely meaningless and rooted in a view of religion as a set of philosophical propositions and claims about God and humanity which can be marked out of ten by an outside examiner.

It is true that the proposition that God is one is a central affirmation in Judaism.[33] But if I play word-association games with the term 'Judaism', the words and images which start to flow are not primarily philosophical propositions or abstract truth-claims. I think of Friday night in my home, the collective endeavour of my workplace, the depth of religious emotion that welled up in me at my son's *bar mitzvah*. Religion for me is about meaning, about encounter and experience, about duty and the realization of goodness. Its truth is to be seen to a significant extent in the ethical and spiritual actuality of its exponents' lives. And there I see both good and bad, true and false. Judaism and Christianity are such complex phenomena, expressed in such a multiplicity of beliefs and credal formulae at different times and in different places by different people, that to devise some kind of scoring system to determine which is propositionally 'better' or 'truer', Judaism or Christianity, speaks more about the anxieties and cultural baggage of the person needing to make the claim than about any real or worthwhile exercise.

The imparative is more useful than the comparative

As Keith Ward says:

> Since God's self-disclosure is co-operative and persuasive, what he reveals will depend partly on what human minds are capable of understanding. God does not blast through our minds with a clear truth out of the blue . . . Our human interests and preoccupations can determine the sorts of disclosures of God we are able to have . . . Not all discernments of God will be equally valid, by any means. But one reason for the variety of divine discernments will be found in the differing temperaments of those who seek to relate to God.[34]

I am a Jew both by birth and by covenantal commitment. Every fibre of me has been shaped by the history and culture that have been handed on to me. They interact with the product of my upbringing in the latter part of the twentieth century, the Jewish cultural inheritance interacting with the Western liberal one to produce the kind of thinking that this chapter reveals. My beliefs and my actions are shaped by who I am, and who I am is profoundly influenced by my birth and upbringing and place in history. That is both my strength and my limitation. As Ward puts it succinctly: 'People will see what their cultural backgrounds and interests enable them to see.'[35]

All of which leads me to understand why I should feel that Judaism works best for me and why I should devote my life to the painful struggle of a minority tradition with the dominant cultural ideas of the day. If I had been born elsewhere or at another time, I would not think and believe precisely as I do. Such truths as I perceive and such beliefs as I hold are shaped by factors other than my own objective analysis alone. I will struggle for truth; I will wrestle with faith; I will do my best, but I am not capable of wholly objective, comparative thinking – I am inevitably a committed player in the game, each stroke a product of coaching as well as autonomous judgment. That is why the value of dialogue is, for me, most brilliantly and accurately summed up by the pioneering Catholic thinker Raimundo Panikkar:

> Once internal dialogue has begun, once we are engaged in a genuine intrareligious scrutiny, we are ready for what I call the *imparative* method – that is, the effort at learning from the other and the attitude of allowing our own convictions to be fecundated by the insights of the other. I argue that, strictly speaking, comparative religion, on its ultimate level, is not possible, because we do not have any neutral platform outside every tradition whence comparisons may be drawn. How can there be a no-man's-land in the land of Man? In particular fields this is indeed possible, but not when what is at stake is the ultimate foundations of human life. We cannot compare (*comparare* – that is, to treat on an equal – *par* – basis), for there is no fulcrum outside. We can only *imparare* – that is, learn from the other, opening ourselves from our standpoint to a dialogical dialogue that does not seek to win or to convince but to search together from our different vantage points.[36]

Religion is a culturally and historically moulded inheritance, a provisional map, a journey, a vessel for fragments of truth, imperfectly perceived. What brings one close to God, what illumines the meaning of life, depends to a considerable extent on where one has come from and who one is. Would I be a more faithful servant of God if I converted to Christianity? Would I have been happier had I become a solicitor rather than a rabbi? Who knows? Who can ever know, since life has been designed to prevent one systematically trying out the different options! I can only work on informed hunches and I am utterly convinced that trading the private language of my particular faith for any other language would be of no advantage to me. The reverse. Judaism is mine – magnificent, obscure, fascinating, frustrating, joyous. Judaism is my home, is part of me. It is, in its countless facets, good and bad, true and false, and interfaith dialogue is of great assistance in weighing, testing and purifying. But better, truer than the faith of some of my Christian dialogue partners? As Panikkar suggests, the question is based upon a false assumption.[37] There are

Christians who describe their Christianity as 'unique' and 'unrepeatable'.[38] Fine. So is my Judaism. An apple and an orange can each be unique and unrepeatable. But, sadly, many go on to insist that Christianity is also 'definitive', 'more truthful than any other' and that Christ is the mediator between God and all human lives.[39] These are unacceptable and repellant conclusions born of a philosophical argument devised to bolster that imperialistic smile which simply does not reflect the reality of faith.

Where our respective maps may join

Jewish religious thinking has a long history which predates Hellenism and Greek philosophy. Later on, Aristotle and Plato were to be understood and used by Jewish religious thinkers, particularly from Saadia in the ninth century onwards. But Judaism was never so influenced or so indebted that it did not retain other modes of thinking. There are many instances in which the rabbis chose to retain truths that they knew to be truths, even though logic saw them as irreconcilable.[40] Judaism has always lived comfortably with a particular paradox about the nature of God. God has been consistently the God of Abraham, Isaac and Jacob – loving and angry, just and compassionate, hiding and revealing, author of the universe yet absurdly concerned with 'this people Israel'.[41] Yet God is also so great that God can only be described in negative terms, as beyond almost all human conception and knowledge. The paradox has been held because both portraits ring true and conform to our spiritual and intellectual experience. The mediaeval Jewish mystics describe the latter God as Ein Sof – Without End. The Kabbalists devised all manner of contortions to explain how the Ein Sof could become Creator and originate the world and humanity. At such points, logic and the language of philosophy are stretched almost to breaking point in order to describe and explain what we know to be true.

The God of Abraham, Isaac and Jacob, indeed of Sarah, Rebekah, Rachel and Leah, is my Jewish God. At times He or She seems curiously parochial and dangerously in my own image and that is something that, both to myself and in dialogue, I freely acknowledge. Christ comes to the dialogue room and I experience him perhaps in something of the same way in which Christians experience the God of Abraham, Isaac and Jacob. Fascinating, perplexing, enlightening, puzzling, distinctive – not my God. And yet, as it were – and paradoxically – an outpouring and an outreaching of the Ein Sof, the 'Without End', whom, I believe, both Jews and Christians address. Not 'the vaguest abstraction from a selection of religious doctrines which have the idea of one perfect reality',[42] but indeed the final ground or nature of everything, that of which we cannot speak directly and objectively because we are limited, culturally conditioned human beings but which we at times are permitted to know is the ultimate reality.

Avoiding 'when you speak of God, you actually mean *my* God'

When Moses asks God to reveal his name,[43] God responds by telling Moses that God is not susceptible to being named. For to name is to control, as all the ancient fairy stories about lamps and genies testify. There is a suspicion in the biblical texts that I quoted earlier of the belief that the nations of the world worship their own gods who are but pale reflections of the true God, named in Judaism. There are similar echoes in the insistence found in certain Christian quarters that 'Christ works through me, even though I know it not' – or, presumably, mediates between God and me, whether I like it or not.[44] I do not wish to fall into the naming, owning trap by suggesting that the God of Abraham, Isaac and Jacob and Christ are both outpourings, faces, manifestations of a God whom Judaism long ago named and owned. 'Our God, we got there first. You worship him, though under a different name.' But I do suggest that the mediaeval Jewish counterbalance to familiarity, God as Ein Sof, points to a recognition of an Unnameable and Unpossessable Greatness at the heart of the universe. We are unable to speak of God except in language that is a reflection of the historical and cultural experience of our traditions. Both Judaism and Christianity, however, have it in them to recognize that which is true and real but which lies beyond the particular scriptures, myths and languages of their own faith.

In dialogue, I journey to the land of my Christian partners and admire, puzzle, study, challenge, value and learn. I go home wiser and inevitably changed. Which many see as risk, but others, myself included, as enrichment. Though I will never cease from pointing out its failings towards my faith and the consequences of teachings I regard as misguided, I have no need to denigrate or condescend. The land is real and true, though, like mine, imperfect. It is no betrayal of my own country to offer respect and honour and recognition of our common source and goal. In the mutual granting of space, ungrudgingly and unreservedly, lies the hope for new growth and insight into the Oneness out of which our purposeful diversity flows.

2. The Geography of Theology

ALBERT H. FRIEDLANDER

The preoccupation with dialogue in our century marks the progress from earlier confrontations and disputations which have taken place between Judaism and Christianity over the centuries. Tony Bayfield's remarks also reflect the very special place of dialogue which he has created at the Sternberg Centre, and are a message to the public at large, to those questioners who search for a religious identity within their faith-group and outside it. This book was written by questioners who are also believers. Tony's theses represent an elegant and compassionate approach to an encounter between faiths desperately in need of the openness which characterizes what he says. Most of what he has to say is eminently acceptable to both partners of the encounter. Nevertheless, there are bound to be aspects of his presentation which must be examined with great care – and perhaps challenged.

We are a people

First of all, though, one must see his comments in context. If there are those who are astonished at the openness of Tony's approach to Christianity, and by the faith he expresses in the dialogue partners, one has to remember who these partners were: fine scholars who could be trusted absolutely. In our discussions there was no need for cautious politeness, circumlocutions or evasions. We agreed to disagree from the very beginning, and these years of discussion among us gave an enduring richness and depth to our faith as we responded to the intellectual and emotional challenges of these encounters. But this was almost too good to be true. In order to expand, we limited ourselves. We Jews talked to those Christians with whom we had most in common, and they in turn met Jewish scholars whose openness had made them participants in most religious discussions within the general community. What would have happened if we had brought Jewish Christians into this group? I do not refer here to 'Jews for Jesus', who perhaps cause as much embarrassment to the Christian community as they cause uneasiness to us. But there are over 9,000 Jews in the United States who become Christians in the course of a year, among them an Episcopal clergywoman and a former schoolmate of mine at the University of Chicago. Unlike Franz Rosenzweig, they did not hesitate at the boundary and turn back; they become devout Christians who had rejected Judaism. I think of the great German church historian Neander (once called Mendel); and I recall long conversations with Ulrich Simon, whose classic book on a Christian theology of Auschwitz impressed me deeply. I know that in theory our discussions with them should not differ from the encounters with the Christians in our dialogue group; in practice, there would be differences.

Why? The answer lies in a dimension of Jewish faith which does differ from our neighbour's affirmations. We are a people. We are part of a covenant which binds us together, and the abandonment of it for a new faith will always hurt us, even when we respect the right of an individual to walk a private way which goes outside our own community. In an intra-faith discussion, I will challenge the fanatical Zionist. When I deal with the essence of Judaism, I rejoice in our universalism. But when I come to the affirmation of Jewish existence, to the proclamation of the Jew as a revelation, as it were, in the world, I cannot exclude the reality of the state of Israel. In an odd way, Christians have come to see this – as they engage in dialogue with us – where our thinking sometimes falters.

Some post-war German theologians have made important advances.[1] Clemens Thoma's *Christian Theology of Judaism*[2] must be noted. David Flusser, an Israeli scholar, in his introduction to that book makes a postulate regarding the Jewish state:

> The Christian theologians of Judaism have to accept that the Jewish understanding of election does not refer to the Jewish religion, but to a human group: Israel – and the people Israel is incomplete without the land.[3]

And Flusser demands to know whether or not there can be a valid Christian theology of the Jew if it does not see the connection with the Jew and the God-given land. There is an awkwardness here, of course. Thoma acknowledges the reality of the Jewish people in their land but surrounds it with so many limitations – some rising out of political worries – that this ceases to be a theological statement. There is also Franz Mussner's *Tractate on the Jews*[4] (which in some ways causes me more worry than Thoma's generous work): Mussner interprets the existence of Israel as a sign 'that God has not abandoned the Jews from His guidance'.[5] I cite the two works as typical of the new attempt by German theologians to understand the theological confrontations with Judaism and Jew out of the context of a history which has its special anguish for them and makes dialogue an almost physical necessity. F. M. Marquardt, in particular, has advanced the cause of dialogue with his writings which have culminated in a new christology based upon her perception of the Jewish people. And Johann Baptist Metz, starting with an early text 'Ecumene after Auschwitz',[6] has been a prophetic voice at the German university with his insistence that 'no Christian theology is valid today which does not begin with Auschwitz!'

These texts are relevant only in so far that they indicate the dynamics of a true conversation between Judaism and Christianity which rise out of a post-Holocaust era; but they also bring us to see some of the complexities which the Manor House Group encountered when Jews and Christians tried to speak about their neighbour's faith based upon a specific revelation. The difference I have tried to stress here resides in the reality of the Jews as a people with a land, a reality linked to Judaism itself. 'Peoplehood' may be less of a problem within Christianity. Yet can one discuss this without being aware that Jewish Christians, in some way, are still part of Israel (the 'Brother Daniel case' of Oscar Rufeisen, for example)?[7] And can the church, with its emphasis upon being the 'Israel of the spirit', ignore the aspect of peoplehood in an attempt to fashion a Christian theology for Jews?

Again a Jewish theology for Christians is today built upon Rosenzweig's vision, but a 'double covenant', with all of its respect for both religious traditions, is in the end a fragmented solution. Its rejection of Islam, for example, becomes a problem half a century later. There is a solid ground for dialogue, of course, in the recognition of the Bible as revealed by God. And, to the extent that the Christian revelation is based upon this Jewish text, Christians can really only deny the Jewish revelation at the expense of their own authenticity.

Perhaps 'peoplehood' should enter the discussion here. Returning to my first worry, I would again indicate that the 'Jewish Christian' still shares in the Jewish people (and that his or her conversion can be voided up to the final moment of life). It does seem to me that our group stopped short in its dialogue. We included discussions on the land of Israel as seen by Jews and Christians, but somehow it made little impact upon our theology. Instead, the issue was treated with great care, as part of a political scene divorced from religious doctrines. One might cite here Clemens Thoma's cautious acknowledgment of the state of Israel:

It must be accepted out of human compassion (*Mitmenschlichkeit*) in the interest of the Jewish people and all of the non-Jews who live in the state of Israel.[8]

A divine *menage à trois*

That is being very cautious; and theology cannot be carried out in cautious words. Somewhere, somehow, absolute statements must be made. This is one of the strengths of Tony's presentation. He does not compromise. The other aspect of such admirable firmness is, of course, that one may not always agree with him. We can accept the analysis of the protagonists of religion speaking a language which is transformed by the partner but still able to share fundamental truths of the religious life. Despite our celebration of secular ethics in a caring society, each one of us saw in himself and herself – and in the other – *homo religiosus*, and this gave the firmest foundation for our encounters. We do not reject secularity; as Jews, we acknowledge it in a particular way. Tony's story of the Anglican minister and the rabbi coming out of their front door to march to their specific place of worship reminded me of Dannie Abse's poem (the same picture, the same locality, north-west London). But Abse (as Heinrich Heine did 150 years earlier) rejects both religious options. Yet the not-to-be-forgotten point remains: Dannie Abse is still a valued member of the Jewish community. If and when we fully come to terms with the intra-religious dialogue of our tradition, it should be easier to achieve this with our neighbours! Yet, again, the warning: those who take part in dialogue are seldom typical of their respective faith communities.

Both religions view the relationship between the worshipper(s!) and God as a marriage relationship; the Hebrew Bible is filled with that insight. Perhaps dialogue would be easier if polygamy had maintained itself as a pattern of social organization. But we've opted for a 'jealous God', and for a jealous people. There are a hundred reasons – and quotations from the Bible – to deflect this pose against the idolaters and the non-believers. Nevertheless, the whole language of love within the realm of religion is an exclusive language. The marriage relationship contains as much jealousy as love. 'Love' itself is a term which divides us: *caritas, agape, eros* – religion cautiously subdivides this passion into controllable areas, bringing us into absolute relationships where no outsiders may enter. To allow the other religion to become a family friend leads to the friction which has generated tragedy in thousands of years of literature (and it did at times seem to me that some of the dialogues held resembled the confrontations of a *ménage à trois*). We can and do accept the other as a passionate lover of God; but this does not bring us beyond Lessing's two-hundred-year-old parable about which of the 'three rings' was authentic.

I realize that this is not enough. The Enlightenment stance of tolerance was an important advance in the field of human relationships. It gave comfort and support to the minorities who, in Herder's simile, were a necessary part of the well-tended garden where many varieties of flowers blended together in a beautiful pattern. For those of us who insist upon revelation as the root of faith, this is at best a partial accommodation to our neighbours. That is also why I worry a bit about the rational way in which both partners have been using biblical criticism as a common ground for faith. We have gone beyond Wellhausen's 'higher antisemitism' (as it was termed by nineteenth-century Jewish scholars), where even that darkness was filled with the lightning flashes of brilliant insights. We feel comfortable and instructed reading Martin Noth, Gerhard von Rad, John Bright and the Scandinavian school with its 'oral transmission' approach which is compatible with Buber. When Tony quotes Keith Ward on biblical narrative as reflecting,

> . . . the sort of relation to God which the final writers and editors felt themselves to have, inextricably intertwined and projected back onto memories of far distant events which have been treasured as founding-events of the Israelite community . . . a superposition of spiritual symbols upon an irrecoverable core of historical memory . . . (p. 21),

I can see myself reflected in that scholarship. And I am still unhappy. Unlike Tony, I cannot see that Judaism and Christianity share a strong tendency to overload the historical (p. 24). Creation, Exodus, and Sinai are both revelation and historical present for me, just as I assume Calvary to occupy the same position for Christianity.

Are these events exclusive of one another? For me, every Passover *Seder* brings me back to my journey out of Egypt – it is recoverable and part of a historical memory which makes *zakhor!* (remember!) a daily act of renewing awareness of revelation. And I also feel, in part supported by what Christians say to me, that Exodus and Sinai are events in the life of the Christian which shape them as individuals and as a group. From the beginning, the rabbis supported a sincere but still 'public relations' project in their stress upon the Noachide Laws[9] in Genesis as the legitimization of non-Jewish relationships to God and the ethical imperatives rising out of this. I still feel uncomfortable with this. The covenant with humanity is contained in creation. The fact that *mitzvot*, (commandment), *mishpatim*, (laws) and the whole rich fabric of *halakhah* (Jewish Law) in the Torah came to be part of the covenant marked upon the very body of the Jew gave us that very specialized marriage-relationship with God which others could not enter in the same way – but neither do Jews enter it in identical fashion! And I *do* therefore feel the Christians to be part of a divine covenant rising out of the creation. The attempt to establish a 'second covenant' through Noah is unnecessary – particularly when one considers the ethical limitations if non-Jews live under that doctrine. Sinai *lives* for Christians, and the words went out in all the languages of the world.

We share the Bible as the book of the revelation, and may leave aside for the moment the differences of interpretation where prefiguration, displacement of Israel by the 'new Israel' and the re-interpretation of messianic texts came to separate us both in history and in theology. In our time, without bringing the Christian community back 'into the fold', we can and must acknowledge their legitimacy as a lawful spouse of God. But then we come to the New Testament. Tony wants to recognize it as a book of revelation. In this, he brings an absolute honesty to the enterprise of dialogue which challenges us to move from pre-conceived stances in our theology. He exposes the hollowness of a rationalist stance which blends tolerance with an approach to the biblical texts now subjected to the rigours of critical scholarship. In that process, the Hebrew Bible and the New Testament do indeed become equals: a Mt Everest and a K2 rising above the mountain ranges of religious literature. But can unique revelation have an equal? There *cannot* be an authentic Christianity which does not recognize Jesus as the risen Christ (*pace* to the border regions of a vast Christian landscape where this doctrine has been abandoned). But Jews do not recognize Jesus as the risen Christ; the challenge of this 'scandal' has passed us by. Tony can only recognize the New Testament as revelation by surrounding the mystery of its core with an enigma which surpasses Jewish understanding; but then the salt of this text loses its flavour.

Tony feels compelled to say that:

. . . Christians find in the life and death of Jesus as described in the New Testament and in the tradition which flows from those events the fullest disclosure of the nature of God and God's will for them. Such faith involves no necessary error or illusion (p. 21).

He feels comfortable with this, but wants to explore its intellectual and religious honesty. I am happy to walk that way with him, but find myself headed towards a different conclusion. The authenticity of the revelation for the Christian rises out of an encounter with the doctrines derived from Hebrew scriptures and the New Testament: the second text is based upon the first. Yet to the Jew who cannot accept the central doctrine of the Christian faith these texts are contradictory. Even in terms of biblical scholarship, they are not the same type of texts. One text was written in the span of a thousand years, the other one within decades. One deals with the flow of history as it courses through Jewish life, and with the gradual revelation of God's will for humanity. The other is a blazing and triumphant declaration of one salvific event: God's son sacrificed at Calvary and risen to give all humans eternal life. It is difficult to accept such a text as sacred when one rejects that message. And yet, curiously enough, when one has turned away from placing the mystery of the New Testament in an affirmation of specific revelation, one does not necessarily deny Christianity.

Judaism has recognized Christianity as a true faith, as proper worship based upon divine revelation, throughout the centuries. We recognize many roads towards salvation, and respect the inner mystery of those ways, looking more towards an outward manifestation of ethical action where those paths parallel ours. It often appears to me that the Christians with whom I have engaged in dialogue are closer to God than I am. I *cannot* judge the New Testament and declare it to be revelation. I *can* and do judge the Christian I meet and can accept that he or she has been addressed by God in a special way, that their life is *filled* with revelation. I felt this when I met Albert Schweitzer; I feel this simply knowing about Mother Teresa; and there are many members in our dialogue group who convince me that when I am near to them I am closer to God.

How, then, do I deal with the New Testament when I recognize that my Christian colleagues are filled with its spirit and cannot be divorced from the text? In a strange way, an inversion of authority takes place: *they* make it authentic because of God's movement through their own lives. A personal revelation exists here, and I honour it even when it remains a mystery. And I am also able to pray alongside of them – in St George's Chapel at Windsor, with the Carmelite nuns in Berlin – even though I cannot pray *with* them: the Christian doctrine of the words pushes me away even as I come closer to their anguished faith. I *do* have a special relationship with the Gospels as well; but it differs from the way in which it serves as their bread of heaven.

I love the Gospels (in spite of the antisemitism which Tony rightly sees in those texts). I love them in the manner and according to the teachings of Leo Baeck, who viewed them as authentic documents of Jewish history written by Jews, about Jews, and initially for Jews. On that level, I have already negated the central part of their message; but they reinforce the Jewish dimension of the man from Nazareth, and give me a deeper understanding of the religious turmoil of that time which Hyam Maccoby describes with such profound scholarship.

I use these texts within my dialogue with the Christian community. Every two years, I participate in the Protestant Kirchentag in Germany, where more than 200,000 Christians come together to explore their faith.

Each time, I do a New Testament text in a dialogic Bible study with a Christian scholar. I try not to let scholarship interfere with the interpretations given by rabbis and church fathers. The texts become a bridge between us, uniting us in the quest for God. And, in that context, recalling the Ruhr Kirchentag of 1991, I can compare texts about healing and link Miriam and Job with the young man healed by Jesus in the Mark text. There is no battle here regarding authority between the Old and New texts. We deal with merited and unmerited suffering, and the dialogue partners instruct one another. In the same way, I generally give one of the sermons for the opening evening of the conference, preaching in a major church. I try to reinforce their Christian faith by giving them a Jewish homily on their text; and we are both relatively happy with the outcome of this encounter.

Praying alongside one another

I know that there are many who do not like our praying 'alongside' one another, let alone 'with' the other. The headline in *The Times*,[10] 'Evangelicals Strive to Close Church Door on Rival Faiths', did not come as a surprise. Over 600 fairly prominent clergymen rallying against interfaith worship and prayer will fight such evils as the Commonwealth Day Observance at Westminster Abbey, and would view the Week of Prayer for World Peace with horror (as it happens, I edited and wrote that prayer pamphlet!). But then, viewing this phalanx of devout Christians, am I not hoist by my own petard? If I see the revelation in devout Christians rather than in their authoritative text, can I encounter it in these honest religionists who reject me? My answer here rests upon the teachings of my revered rabbi and instructor Leo Baeck, who encountered the divine in the polarities of mystery and commandment: there is no true revelation experience if the mystery does not contain ethical imperatives, the commandment; and the commandment, in turn, leads through the neighbour to the divine mystery. I will *not* say that the evangelical priest who cannot acknowledge my religious dimension is an unethical person; but his jealous, zealous love of God obscures any message he wants to bring to me. This is the tragedy of the Christian 'decade of evangelism': it obscures and destroys Christian teachings by taking them outside the realm of dialogue. A Christian who testifies for God to me by acts of loving kindness awakens my realization that God speaks through him. A preacher of dogma who only wants to press the seal of his unique vision on my brow cannot reach me. A Chasidic rebbe, chanting the liturgy of Yom Kippur afternoon describing the service of the High Priest in the Jerusalem Temple, would change the language from 'then he said' to 'then I said' – he felt he had been the High Priest in a previous incarnation. But I do not stand in the Holy of Holies, and I cannot follow a Christian into his mysteries. Is there, perhaps, an 'outer court for Jews'? I do not really want to know.

This much I know: when Sister Louis Gabriel, our beloved Charlotte Klein of the Sisters of Sion, died after a loving ministry and witnessing for God, I participated in the funeral and the interment together with Rabbi Lionel Blue; and I felt close to God and to the Christian mystery – perhaps even more because of her Jewish dimension. She also taught me that the anti-Judaism in the New Testament did not destroy these texts. It was the combination of the teaching of contempt as developed over the centuries within Christianity which created and preserved murderous antisemitism; but this brings me back to the Bible.

Ralph Ingersoll, a militant atheist, wallowed in what he termed 'the mistakes of the Old and New Testament', and some still delight in accusing the Torah of genocidal instructions regarding the Canaanites. These texts are there, just as there are the hateful stories in the New Testament. Yet if those mountains of the holy land in their fiery explosions deposited the slag and lava of human hatred as encrustations upon the slopes of the Holy Mountain, one must not mistake the dross for the gold – the messengers of the king have always added their imperfections to the precious words that were given to them. Just as I see the revelation in the person, so I see the flaws. The New Testament, like my Hebrew Bible, becomes the place of encounter. And there are times when we come back with a different message from the Holy Mountain. But I am not Moses, and Richard Harries is not Paul or Peter. Citizens of the last decades of the twentieth century, we meet as on Dover Beach, we watch the sea of faith go out and we reassure one another of the nature of the religious enterprise.

The suffering God

The most significant aspect of our interfaith dialogue over these past years was our discussion of the concept of the suffering God in Judaism and in Christianity. Here, we came to understand that human suffering is the paradigm of divine suffering – not the other way round. The Christian's approach usually starts with the suffering on the cross. This incomprehensibility would only enter human understanding when seen in the context of human suffering. Here is where Auschwitz became relevant to christology, more even than the suffering Shekinah who went into exile with her children driven out of the Holy Land. This is also the link which permits us to pray alongside one another, and to see how we can and do enrich our lives by this blessing of dialogue. In the end, that is why I feel compassion for the poor Evangelicals who are trapped in the romantic areas of their faith which will not permit them to break through into the classic areas of rational discourse where the other is no longer a means to an end, but an end in itself.

Almost two decades ago, I attended a world conference on religion in Los Angeles where over 200 papers were given. I gave my paper on the Shoah and had an encounter with Richard Rubenstein, an American Jewish 'Death of God' theologian, which was the beginning of a long relationship of learning with that dark and brilliant master. But then, in due course, I tired of the tumult of scholarship. While the others dutifully trudged from one talk to the next one, I jumped into the swimming pool. At the other end, a similar spirit plunged into the pool, and we passed each other in the middle, nodding gravely. He was by far the better swimmer, and in the end caught me so that we swam side by side. Then, we climbed out; and, for the next hour, Raimundo Panikkar and I entered into a talk that became a dialogue and a positive confrontation. I was therefore particularly pleased to see Tony's quotation from Raimundo Panikkar regarding the 'imparative method' – the way of imparting knowledge to one another. As he stated, we cannot compare one another when we both start with the ultimate foundations of human life which we have approached in our unique ways. *Imparare*, to learn from one another, is always possible.

That is what is happening between Jews and Christians, and what may yet happen between us and Muslims. Trapped in the midst of the human imperfections which create war, poverty and suffering, we understand enough about the nature of our enterprise to recognize that there is no solution independent of dialogue with our neighbour. Beyond that conversation lies our dialogue with God which is of necessity stormy and imperfect. The question of theodicy, covered elsewhere in this book, then arises. Our separate traditions recognize that God cannot be placed before the bar of human justice. Yet such a scene becomes part of the drama of our diverse approaches, whether in Dostoyevski's Grand Inquisitor scene or in the biblical Job. In our time, God is tried by the suffering prisoners of Schamgorod and found guilty.[12] Then, the trial over, the prisoners go to evening prayers.

The geography of theology is marked by a retreating boundary which makes our quest a *theologia viatorum* where travellers can recognize one another along the way. Some of the stages I noticed along my own journey can be summarized at this point:

1. As David Flusser said: 'Election does not refer to the Jewish religion, but to a human group, Israel – and the people Israel is incomplete without the land.'

2. We are the people of the book: *our* book, the Hebrew Bible. A

Christian challenge to this text challenges Christians' own authenticity. The New Testament speaks to them with greater clarity when they see the Hebrew dimensions contained in it.

3. We recognize each other as *homo religiosus*, and I find the revelation of a true faith more in the individual Christian I encounter than in the texts the Christian venerates and which I respect from some distance.

4. The covenant is a love relationship, which I see as a marriage. I live it in a monogamous way, and see the Christian experiencing the same wonder. It is one of many reasons why I see their revelation in the person rather than in the text, particularly when the faith is expressed by ethical action.

5. I can and do pray alongside the Christian and can join Christians in worship. The fact that I have reservations about the texts means that I cannot fully enter their experience of the liturgy: it would be a lessening, an adulteration of their faith for me to plunge into it without reservation.

6. In the end, I see ourselves united by the covenant of creation, and feel uncomfortable with the 'covenant of Noah': *all* humanity is united by the Revelation of Genesis which comes to us in the Torah and makes us responsible for the world.

Our group has journeyed together for a while, and is now dispersing, but not separating. We have shared our sorrows, including the awareness of the Holocaust where Christians died alongside Jews in the concentration camps. We are then linked by memories of that darkness – I would never want Jews to claim a monopoly in suffering! – but we are also joined in the hope for a messianic kingdom.

3. Exploring Unmapped Territory

MARGARET SHEPHERD

Mutual esteem

Gamaliel's words to the Sanhedrin concerning the arrested apostles in Acts 5.38–39 remain valid: 'Leave these men alone! Let them go! For if their purpose or activity is of human origin, it will fail. But if it is from God, you will not be able to stop these men; you will only find yourselves fighting against God.' That such words remain equally valid in the other direction, with regard to the persistence of Judaism's faithful witness to God throughout the centuries of Christian persecution, is only being recognized and valued in our own time. The process of mutual esteem, of mutual appreciation of each other's 'purpose or activity' being 'from God', of God and God-directed, has properly, if tentatively, begun. The steps taken, if relatively few so far, are irreversible. It is possible that most Jews and Christians are as yet unready to work through the implications of real acknowledgment of the other, but some must lead the way with courage. Rabbi Tony Bayfield is one of these.

One might ask, 'Who are the partners in dialogue?'

Individuals, certainly, but individuals need to stand also within their community. Is it too soon, perhaps, to be at the stage of communities in dialogue – the kind of dialogue envisaged here? For it is true to say that we are in the minority in our respective faith communities, we Christians and Jews who are making serious attempts to break new ground in the dialogue process, who are striving to create theological space for the other. Given our shared, painful history as Jews and Christians, I greatly admire the brave stance of Tony's paper where he challenges the common Jewish supposition that Christianity was 'founded upon a mistake' (p. 20), where he is prepared to acknowledge the Christian scriptures as a book of revelation, with 'God . . . present in those events, words and symbols whatever the complexities and flaws of transmission, redaction and interpretation' (p. 22).

40

In the dialogue experience new questions are being asked of our faith, which is suddenly vulnerable and no longer triumphalistic, knowing all the answers. Such vulnerability can lead to a sense of discomfort, nakedness, yet excitement at the potential, for we are on the brink of virgin, unexplored territory. The future demands openness, courage, absolute honesty and humility. We're in this together. Both our faith traditions have their inherent, traditional problematics, such as the Jewish sense of 'chosenness' and the Christian belief in the 'uniqueness' of Christ. To question these seriously is disconcerting for both Jew and Christian respectively.

Tony quotes George Steiner with his proposal that the Jewish people 'may have chosen Him' (p. 23) and says of his own Judaism that it, too, is 'unique' (p. 27). So tables may be turned, truth-claims questioned. He reminds us of the sad fact that around some dialogue tables both Christians and Jews may still think, 'My religion is best' (p. 24). I think he is misguidedly over-generous when he says: 'That the Christian participants acknowledge Judaism as of independent salvific value and that they are prepared to acknowledge that Jews can be left to be Jews is not a prerequisite for dialogue' (pp. 20f.). I disagree. It is an absolute prerequisite, though I concede that, if absent at the beginning, it might, hopefully, be the *result* of honest dialogue. Necessary, too, is the established and recognized equality of dialogue partners, noted in Tony's quotation from Rosemary Ruether, who questions whether the Jewish sense of 'distinctiveness' truly allowed the distinctiveness of others to be 'on the same level before God as that of their one "chosen" people' (p. 19). Both Jews and Christians have deep-seated problems in allowing the other to be other, of equal worth, with an equally valid revelation and means of salvation.

Tony points to unspoken agendas in the dialogue scenario, with, sometimes, remaining and persistent Christian and Jewish basic mutual contempt, despite the readily exchanged smiles. He points also to the Jewish 'indifference to the spiritual life of others' (p. 20). Such inversion, readily understood as a result of history, has to be challenged and changed by the witness of Christian self-criticism as the latter relinquishes once and for all its 'triumphant imperialism'. He rightly cites the background of Jewish anger over the history of persecution and forced conversion, both still present in the Christian world, in the guise of antisemitism and missionary activity aimed at the Jews: two sides of the same coin. These have seriously to be addressed by Christians, taking full account of Jewish feeling. The American theologian Paul van Buren, when expounding the church's calling to be of 'service to Israel', to which I shall refer more fully later, speaks of Christian mission to Jews as a 'contradiction',[1] and 'self-defeating',[2] for Christian mission – and mission is integral to its very being – is none other than the mission of the God of Israel. The church would lose its very identity, he says, if it were successful in its 'attempt to rid the world of Jews'.[3] For, 'A God of Israel who had lost its Israel, the God of the covenant who had lost the covenant partner, could hardly be the God who had called together a Gentile church in fulfilment of a part of his promise to Abraham and in confirmation of all his promises to his people Israel.'[4]

Creating theological space is only a first step

Whilst I appreciate the centrality of 'creating theological space' for the other, that, though enormous and crucial, is but a first step. It is not simply a case of 'moving over and making room' for those who are 'not like us', but being prepared to become something very different, something which we perhaps have yet to imagine, something which most people, I suspect, are not yet ready for. The Dominican Jacques Pohier says as much when he faces the issues clearly: 'How does one recognize the religious value of the other religions without devaluing the unique role of Jesus Christ in the encounter between God and human beings? How does one stress the unique role of Jesus Christ in this encounter without devaluing the real religious worth of the other religions?'[5] He points to a problem: 'At present, . . . Christianity formulates and proclaims the absolutely unique role of Jesus Christ in the revelation of God by means of categories which it has inherited from former centuries; however, these categories were not developed in connection with this problem and do not allow it to be resolved.'[6] We are in a new situation requiring new, creative answers.

Pohier further outlines the dilemma for Christians:

> Are we here . . . condemned to 'all or nothing'? Must we practise a terrorism which consists in refusing all religious value to other religions (except in so far as they anticipate or participate in Christianity) in order to preserve the originality of the role of Jesus Christ as the revelation of God? Or are we condemned to reducing Jesus Christ to the level of being no more than a great religious genius of humanity in order to respect the religious value of these other religions? In the present state of our thinking this dilemma would seem to be inescapable. But the absurdity of the dilemma shows that our way of thinking must change, even if we do not yet know how.[7]

He tentatively suggests,

> Is it not in Jesus Christ himself that we shall find a possible principle of coexistence between two groups which seem contradictory to our present

way of thinking: on the one hand the proclamation by faith of the radical and plenary decision of Jesus Christ for God and of the radical and plenary commitment of God in his revelation in Jesus Christ, and on the other hand respect for radical and plenary decisions of another kind for God, and for the radical commitment of God in these other revelations which are realized in these other decisions? Can Christianity perhaps find its truth and that of Jesus Christ otherwise than to be arrogating a more or less explicit monopoly of divine revelation? I do not know the answer, and . . . we shall probably need several generations to find it.[8]

We do not have the answers. We are searching together for a way to be together, to affirm each other, truthfully and sincerely. Perhaps Pohier is right that it will take 'several generations', but, as the second century Rabbi Tarfon said, so many, many generations ago, in another context: 'The day is short, and the work is great, and the labourers are sluggish, and the wages are high, and the Master of the house is insistent. It is not your duty to finish the work, but nor are you free to desist from it.'[9]

No easy answers

Some theologians have tried to address the difficulties. There are no easy answers. Inclusivism. Exclusivism. Pluralism. All have been tried – and, to my mind, found wanting. Both Raimundo Panikkar and the Indian Christian Samartha reject the traditional understanding of the definitive normativity of Christ.[10] There has been a call to balance christocentrism and theocentrism. The American Catholic theologian Paul Knitter, like many others, questions Christ as God's definitive, normative revelation: 'The experience of faith necessarily includes the conviction that Jesus *is* God's revelation and grace. It does not necessarily include the conviction that he *alone* is this revelation and grace.'[11] Therein lies the tension.

Tony rightly questions Knitter's final words: 'Perhaps Jesus the Nazarene will stand forth (without being imposed) as a unifying symbol, the universally fulfilling and normative expression, of what God intends for all history.'[12] I, too, would question them. It might be that Knitter felt that he had, after all, given away too much in the course of the book, as he struggled with the paradox of the seemingly impossible. It might also be the case that we should be leaning heavily on the word 'perhaps' in the concluding statement which Tony finds difficult and contradictory. That is only one possible scenario. Knitter has boldly painted others, without drawing any watertight conclusions. Elsewhere he has stressed that 'the essence of being a Christian is *doing* the will of the Father rather than knowing or insisting' on the uniqueness of Jesus[13] – and that 'theologians who are exploring a pluralist theology of religions and a nonabsolutist christology . . . want to be faithful to the original message of the Nazarene – that to which Jesus always subordinated himself: the kingdom of love, unity, and justice'.[14]

I repeat: there are no neat, ready-made answers. The Catholic missionary theologian David Bosch recognizes this. What we need, he says, is 'a theology of religions characterized by creative tension, which reaches beyond the sterile alternative between a comfortable claim to absoluteness and arbitrary pluralism.'[15] There must be 'room for embracing the abiding paradox of asserting both ultimate commitment to one's own religion and genuine openness to another's, of constantly vacillating between certainty and doubt'.[16] We are indeed, as Bosch says, 'dealing with a mystery'.[17] In another, but related context, Tony reminds us that 'God is not susceptible to being named', that there is 'an Unnameable and Unpossessable Greatness at the heart of the universe' (p. 28). We must be aware of the holiness of the ground upon which we tread, and tread softly, with reverence. We simply must leave room for mystery. Is it not a *chutzpah* to think that we either have all the answers to these questions, or, indeed, ever will have? At the last analysis, God is greater than all of us.

God may be recognized in the dialogue

God may, however, be recognized in the dialogue, may be found in the other, in the religious tradition of the other. The American rabbi Leon Klenicki outlines the movement involved:

> Essentially, the desire to relate to the other as a person of faith emerges out of recognition and understanding of the other's value, specifically in the case of Christianity, in acceptance of its covenantal destiny and mission. It is also my own acceptance of my mission, the actualization of God's covenant in daily existence as a living vocation . . . I am totally in covenantal relationship with God when I accept the other in covenant with God, the Christian.[18]

Here Rabbi Klenicki and Tony meet in their affirmation of the validity of the Christian's covenant with God, the revelation from God within Christianity. So there is an essential, two-way process: *backwards* to our own faith tradition in which we are steeped and to which we are committed, to examine it courageously, honestly; *forwards* to relate creatively to the other, our partner in dialogue: 'The history of the Church shows that elements in the tradition contain the seeds of becoming something different.'[19] A circular movement, perhaps, with the circumference becoming ever greater and bolder in its dimension, yet the distance to 'the still point' becoming less and less. Tony quotes God as saying 'both to me and my neighbour, "*Gey gesundaheit*", "Go in my service in peace" ' (p. 17). I would like to place some Hebrew beside the Yiddish: '*Lech l'shalom*', with the reminder that *this* should strictly be translated as 'Go *towards* peace', rather than 'Go *in* peace'. That should characterize our dialogue, which must be a shared journey towards the God of peace as we move towards each other in reconciliation, understanding and unconditional acceptance of the other *as other*.

The dialogue movement towards God is essentially one of humility, where we lay ourselves open in all vulnerability to the possibility, as Tony rightly says, of being changed ourselves. It leads to a renewed commitment and deepening of our own faith, based on respect for those who have gone before us in that faith – 'even if we have reason to be acutely embarrassed by their racist, sexist, and imperialist bias'.[20] When proposing his 'warrant for redrawing the map', Tony speaks of such a past 'with its different mind-set and agenda' (p. 17). We must heed his warning that it 'should not be manipulated dishonestly to suit contemporary needs' (ibid.). True, and a timely warning, but true, too, is his encouragement to look for 'fingerprints' in the traditions that we have inherited, in order to understand ourselves today. One of these fingerprints, of whose existence some Christians are unaware, and which others do not explore sufficiently, are the different christologies in the Christian scriptures. Tony makes perceptive reference to these when he says that dialogue has helped him to 'understand better what Christians mean . . . that Christians mean many different things' (p. 23) in their interpretation of those scriptures. I suggest that it would be a step forward and a challenge for both Jews *and* Christians to acknowledge this primary diversity of Christianity.

Tony makes a daring, considered statement: '. . . I feel compelled to say . . . I believe that many Christians find in the life and death of Jesus . . . and in the tradition which flows from those events the fullest disclosure of the nature of God and God's will for them. Such faith involves no necessary error or illusion' (p. 21). I more than suspect that this will be too much for most of Tony's fellow-Jews. He is laying his life on the line here. Included, I presume, in that 'tradition', though not explicitly named by Tony, is the Christian belief, however it is understood, in the resurrection of Jesus: that Jesus lives.

The Christian vocation

Paul van Buren,[21] dwelling on this, stresses the Christian's obligation to continue Jesus' service of the Jewish people as spoken of in Rom 15.8–9:

'Christ has become a servant of the Jews (lit.: 'circumcised') on behalf of God's truth, to confirm the promises made to the patriarchs so that the Gentiles may glorify God for his mercy . . .' To serve Israel *as* Israel is the Christian's proper concern, says van Buren, *including* its present-day realities: its return to the land of Israel, its struggle to come to terms with the memories of the Shoah – and I would stress that Christians must recognize both of these to be vital, essential elements of Jewish self-understanding in the twentieth century, and appreciate that real dialogue can only take place with these elements playing a deeply significant role.[22] This, for me as a Sister of Sion, reminds me of the Constitutions of my Congregation: 'Our vocation gives us a particular responsibility to promote understanding and justice for the Jewish Community . . .'[23] This is none other than continuing the work of Jesus who lives.

In the light of Vatican II, the church is 'concerned . . . to affirm the covenant between God and the Jewish people, and to do so clearly in its central confession of faith'.[24] This is a *living* covenant, of course, which has never been revoked by God. It is unfinished, just as 'the Church's Christology is and must remain unfinished . . . because it is evident that God is not yet finished with what he intends in the matter of the relationship between the Church and the Jewish people'.[25]

That conscientization is also part of Sion's vocation, for Constitution 14, speaking of our vocation, continues, saying that it is '. . . to keep alive in the Church the consciousness that, in some mysterious way, Christianity is linked to Judaism from its origin to its final destiny'.[26]

The Vatican 'Notes'[27] speak of both Christians and Jews as 'peoples' of God, the God of Israel. It follows that we are co-workers in God's cause. We have, as van Buren says, a common goal of 'an eventual reign of God's peace and justice on earth',[28] though not a common vision of attaining that goal. 'Truth may be one, as God is one, but the Church and the Jewish people stand in – have been called to – different relationships to the one God.'[29] Such a common goal is hinted at by Tony when he says, 'I find my Christian partners dedicated to the realization of a familiar goodness and prompted by a revealing metaphysical Reality which points to a coincidence of ultimate truths' (p. 24). This he spells out in a note: 'The coincidence is . . . first theological, in the God whom each faith ultimately addresses. Secondly, ethical, in the pursuit of justice and compassion, the search for love and peace . . . in the dialogue encounter there is more than a suspicion of . . . ultimate truths' (n. 31, p. 165).

Over the past 2,000 years we have experienced three distinct stages, outlined by van Buren.[30] There was a moment, all too short-lived, when the church existed *within* Israel, before each, tragically, went its separate way. Since then, with some rare and beautiful exceptions, the story has been of the church *against* Israel. It is only in our own lifetime that we have witnessed the momentous gear-shift. We now face the exciting prospect of the church living at peace and working *with* Israel, in equal partnership in our troubled world which so needs our joint witness to our God.

For the Christian, the ultimate goal, of course, which transcends all discussion of uniqueness, exclusivity, particularity, is that which is expressed in I Cor. 15.28, when Christ's work – which is still in process in his followers – is done: 'then the Son himself will be made subject to him who put everything under him, *so that God may be all in all*'. This may be a goal with which a Jew could feel comfortable. With all the present concern to balance christocentrism and theocentrism, it should not be forgotten that Jesus never takes the place of God in the New Testament – the whole thrust and *raison d'être* of his life and mission was God-centred, God-directed, albeit in deep awareness of a special – what most Christians would want to call unique – relationship with God as Father.

Tony cites Christian belief in the Incarnation itself as a major stumbling block for Jews. However that is expressed, however christology itself is expressed, there remains van Buren's ground rule: 'Every proper Christological statement, however "high", will make clear that it gives glory to God the Father.'[31] Similarly, 'Every proper Christological statement will make clear that it is an affirmation of the covenant between God and Israel.'[32] The living reality of Jesus, begun within Israel's scriptures, Israel's covenant, unfolds together with the unfolding of Israel's living reality, including the present and the future, as well as the past. We need a christology for the Jewish-Christian relationship of *today*, which will 'help the Church to think about this and to find a confession of Jesus Christ appropriate to him today and tomorrow'.[33]

Exploring unmapped territory

This echoes Tony's words: 'The existential reality demands a change in the theology which describes and explains that reality' (p. 17). A *real* meeting between Jews and Christians will, at the end of the day, challenge our theology, both of our own faith and its relation to the other. It will call for a radical change, an entry into new, *unmapped* territory, thus going beyond Tony's image of 'What place do I give to these people in my map of faith?' (p. 15). I suggest that the map has to be set aside – or perhaps recharted, based on a re-examination of tradition, in an entirely fresh way, requiring that 'new word' of Klenicki: 'To relate religiously is to fathom the mystery of our commitments under God and in a dialogue relationship until a new word will be developed to describe the very meaning of the

47

present encounter.'[34] I suggest that it is this *new word* that we must seek to formulate, then use to redesign our religious, ethical and social lives, especially in relation to each other. It is *imperative* that, as Tony says, 'after two thousand years, we try to move on' (p. 20). And the moving on has to be by mutual consent, with mutual commitment at the deepest level, each ready to '*imparare* . . . learn from the other, opening ourselves from our standpoint to a dialogical dialogue that does not seek to win or to convince but to search together from our different vantage points' (p. 26).

Is the 'granting of space' important? Yes. Must it be done 'ungrudgingly'? Yes. 'Unreservedly' (p. 28)? This I believe to be the most important of all, for both Jew and Christian.

I leave the last word with Martin Buber, who said:

The faith of Judaism and the faith of Christendom are by nature different in kind, each in conformity with its human bias and they will indeed remain different, until mankind is gathered from the exiles of the 'religions' into the Kingship of God. But an Israel striving after the renewal of its faith through the rebirth of the person and a Christianity striving for the renewal of its faith through the rebirth of nations would have something as yet unsaid to say to each other and a help to give to one another – hardly to be conceived at the present time.[35]

Buber wrote this in 1951. Forty years on let us dare to conceive it.

Part Two
Text, Tradition and Historical Criticism

4. Text and Tradition: Eating One's Cake and Having It

JOHN BOWDEN

Informal dialogue

For me, much of the more formal interfaith dialogue, whether in written form or in its more official versions, is all too abstract and clinical. Paradoxically, it most resembles the work of scientists, whose activity is based on the premise that our many personal interests in the world, or other aspects of life outside the scientific process, are irrelevant to the work in hand. (And that, incidentally, makes me wonder whether much interfaith dialogue is not perhaps far more infected by attitudes from the modern world than most of those engaged in it realize.) The advantages of more informal dialogue, off the record and by its nature leading to openness, trust and, most important of all, friendship and affection for the other for his or her own sake, is that it makes it impossible to establish any 'no-go' areas. Of course, achieving this atmosphere takes time: what is most important to oneself is often so private that it will be quite some while before one feels able to talk about it to those who once were strangers with a different perspective; and similarly, what is most important to partners and friends in dialogue does not come to the surface immediately.

In this informal dialogue of which we now have a good deal of experience, one of the interesting things which emerges when some of the barriers start to come down and the discussion loosens up is the recognition that some Christians (not all) and some Jews (not all) have already been engaged for even longer in a complex dialogue, if not controversy, with their own tradition. Because of this, generalizations about belief or practice labelled 'Jewish . . .', 'Christian . . .' or 'Jews . . .', 'Christians . . .' become problematical. They provoke the at least unspoken reaction 'but I don't,' or even 'But that's precisely what I've been fighting against in my own tradition for ages'. Of course there is a difference: because of its history, geographical spread and sheer weight of numbers, Christianity has become almost a series of faiths rather than a faith, with very blurred edges indeed in the modern Western world; in Judaism there is clearly a much more solid, hard-core sense of belonging, simply by the fact of being born a Jew; what seems to the non-Jew to be a primal solidarity, reinforced by much suffering and by specific hopes. Nevertheless, the point of differences *within traditions* needs to be made, because it is crucial to understanding our position as believers, whether we like it or not. We live in a very complicated world, with a very complicated and difficult development behind us, and if we try to escape from the consequences by being simplistic, we are doing just that – escaping. Closed communities, ignoring vital developments that are going on around them, may be supportive and may be able to assert themselves, but they achieve this by becoming 'ideologies' in the bad sense of the word; that is, groups whose interpretation of themselves and the world is unwittingly distorted through practical concerns for power and position.

So in theory, the better dialogue becomes, the more complex it is going to get, because none of those involved in it will be simple people, nor will they be speaking from simple backgrounds or situations. But in practice, happily, sometimes things don't work out quite like that. In practice, sometimes, the better dialogue becomes, the simpler it can get, because things which in theory seemed complex prove not to be as complicated as expected, or at least prove not to be major problems *at the level of interfaith dialogue*.

Here's an illustration of what I mean.

It is not at all easy for a Church of England clergyman to live and work in London for any length of time at a job (in my case theological publishing) which takes him out of the established parish system and at the same time find a happy relationship with the local church. For a whole set of reasons which we need not go into here, there is a tension between his status as an ordained priest not attached to a parish and the structures of traditional parish life which find it very difficult to accommodate him. So Sunday is often not a very satisfactory day. It is a consolation to know from other Christians in the same position that this is by no means an isolated problem. But it is even more encouragement to find that *rabbis* living and working in London for any length of time at a job which takes them out of the established synagogue system have precisely the same feeling. That recognized, it is possible to see and accept the problem in much wider terms.[1] It can be seen as a minor instance of the consequence of the forces which shape church life *and* synagogue life alike, forces which can plausibly be studied and illuminated through a sociological approach which is not part of either Judaism or Christianity but which is a now indispensable part of our contemporary world. This new sociological perspective may not make any contribution to actually improving matters, but there is no doubt about the help in *understanding* that it can bring. At least we have a better, more effective, grasp of the problem, even if we have to go on living with it.

The impact of sociology

Over the past decade and more, the sociology which comes into play in this situation has been extended very widely indeed. There are sociological studies of the formation of the people of Israel at the time of the settlement in Palestine,[2] and sociological studies of many periods thereafter, with a particular focus on the period around the time of Jesus, the formation of the early church and the split between Christianity and Judaism after the fall of Jerusalem in 70 CE.[3] As a result of these studies we can follow the changing structure of the Jewish people and their beliefs, and see how the stage was set for the tragedies of the first century of our era which led to the existence of two faiths, in fact sharing so much but taking such different ways.[4] Christians in particular can see how distorted and ideological are many features in their account of the parting of these ways and, not least prompted by Jewish scholars, can see the Jewishness of Jesus and how he can be best understood in the light of the movements and issues of his day.[5] A sociological approach which brings out the differences between Pharisees as they were (and not as they are presented in the Gospels) and Sadducees as they were, and the differing relationships of the two parties to the Roman authorities (and to Jesus) can do much to provide the basis of a reinterpretation of the circumstances of Jesus' crucifixion and those who were responsible for it.[6] A sociological approach can look at the implications for Judaism of the destruction of Jerusalem and for Christianity of the virtual extermination of Jewish Christianity in Palestine and the shift of its activity to the cities of the Hellenistic world.[7]

Most of all, a sociological approach can call attention to the factors which led to the creation of the kind of Christianity which came to dominate the world after Constantine's rise to become ruler of the Roman West in 312 and his official endorsement of Christianity as a state religion.[8] We can see the pressures which led Christians to create a canonical collection of scriptures in imitation of the Hebrew Bible, which became the Old Testament in contrast to the 'New' Testament, and we can see the various factors (by no means purely intellectual or theoretical or devotional, but also political) which led to the formation of a mainstream church to the exclusion of other groups and the gradual establishment of a formidable, binding, structure of dogma, including the doctrines of the Trinity (three persons in one substance) and Incarnation (Jesus Christ is both God and man).[9]

With a sociological approach we can look at all these things. And since we are human, and human beings have an insatiable curiosity, having seen (approximately, at any rate) how one thing happened after another and how, and to what degree, both Jews and Christians are victims of human failings and blindness, we can ask ourselves: Did it all have to be like this?[10] Unless we have a very strange view of God indeed, we shall conclude that what happened in the first centuries of the common era was no divinely determined course but a consequence of the freedom that we have been given. If only we could go right back to one of the points at which things started to go so wrong, and begin again in a different way!

But here we are moving into the realm of daydreams. The fluidity of historical developments at any one time hardens into the facts and structures which are left behind by what actually happens, and these have an ongoing life of their own and influence what is to come. Christians have a Bible, they have doctrines, and they have churches with their particular patterns of order and roles in society, all of which now are what they are, exercising the power not only of beloved aspects of faith but also of established authorities. Jews have their history, often on the underside of Christianity or developing over against it, with its loyalty to God as revealed in the Torah.

Scripture and doctrines are historically conditioned

The great split *within* Judaism and *within* Christianity nowadays is between those who see Bible, doctrine, ministry, Torah or whatever as givens around which everything else revolves, and those who are so aware of the changes that have been brought by modern understanding, and particularly the historical consciousness that has arisen over the past two centuries (of which the sociological approach outlined above is one aspect), that they must give it a major place in their thinking about belief.

Here we seem to be in a period of flux, if not confusion, with the temptation to leave these all too complicated questions, often requiring a good deal of very detailed investigation, on one side. 'Oh no, not that again', has been one common reaction to any suggestion that our group should take one more look at the nature of historical criticism. Partly because of the way biblical criticism in particular has been practised over the last century, and especially over the last decade, the critical approach is thought to be dry, negative, pedantic and irrelevant. And the reaction of the group, particularly the Christians in it, is the reaction of the churches writ small.

There is reluctance to go into detailed examination, which tends to be expected to be arid and negative, but many believers, both Jews and

Christians, are all too often prepared to enjoy any benefits that the modern critical approach may put their way. They will accept new insights which seem to contribute positively to our understanding of religious tradition, some of which I outlined above, but are less prepared to pay the price of these insights, which is a challenge to most of the old-established doctrinal tradition and traditional structure of their faith.

One obvious example of this attempt to eat one's cake and have it seems to me to be the literary approach to the Bible, which has been, and still is, extremely popular among both Jews and Christians. The Bible, it has been discovered, is a good story; theology is also a good story, to be enjoyed and studied as literature. There is a good deal of truth in such a claim, particularly if it is seen as a reaction to the proof-texting of which there has been all too much in the past, and the approach of so-called 'narrative theology' to the biblical text can be as illuminating in its different way as that of sociology. However, it is surely little more than an aesthetic luxury unless it interacts, and *challenges*, the traditional approach to sacred texts and the authoritarian claims that go with that approach. As became evident from around the middle of the last century, if the Bible is to be read in the same way as other books,[11] and illuminated by the techniques (whether historical criticism or literary criticism) which can be applied to other books, then the question of the distinctive revelation, authority, or whatever, of the Bible becomes an urgent problem. If, as one classic modern approach to the Bible, Gabriel Josipovici's *The Book of God*, argues, we should think about the Bible as a person rather than a book, and be concerned to encounter it, as we do persons, rather than decipher it, what does that mean for the traditional view of authority attached to it by Jew or Christian in their different ways? Surely this authority, and all its consequences for the structure of Judaism and Christianity, does not remain in one compartment, and the literary-critical approach in another.

Josipovici goes on:

The closer we are to a person the more certain we will be that we cannot tell his story. Yet we also know that we will never be likely to confuse that person with anyone else, even a close relative . . . Looked at in this way, the Bible can be seen to be unique not because it is uniquely authoritative but because it is itself and not something else. Jubilees and Ecclesiasticus may be its brothers, the Koran, *Paradise Lost* and *Joseph and His Brothers* its cousins, once or twice removed, and so may the works of Homer and Sophocles, Kafka and Celan and Proust. They share certain gestures and expressions, but no one who had once got to know them would ever mistake one for the other.[12]

The revolutionary challenge which that puts to traditional understanding of the Bible, in both Christianity and Judaism, is staggering to contemplate, yet it is being contemplated less and less. Right at the beginning of this century the great German theologian Ernst Troeltsch realized quite clearly that once one embarks on a historical-critical approach there is no turning back, and the same thing goes for literary criticism, which is a younger relative. 'Give it (historical criticism) your little finger,' he said, and it will require your whole hand', adding wryly that in that way it resembled the devil.[13] There is a price to be paid for the benefits that historical, sociological, literary criticism can bring, namely an undermining of past understandings of 'holy books', of Torah or doctrine, and all the religious structures, practices and forms of worship that they legitimate. The demand to pay that price seems to be woven into our nature as twentieth-century human beings; we may not be able to afford the price, or see on what terms we can pay it, but unless we accept the obligation in principle, we shall inevitably suffer – by the fragmentation of our innermost self at the point where it is called on to be most authentic – in our quest for the ways of the God who comes to meet us.

Yet, as I have indicated, there is a constant reluctance to come to terms with the issues here; it is as though attempts keep being made to postpone the day of reckoning. I shall illustrate the point from the development of historical criticism in Christianity; the story in Judaism would be rather different, but not completely so.

Within Christian circles, despite a great deal of opposition, historical criticism of the Bible became established within the churches to the extent of forming part of the training of clergy and, during the twentieth century, even shaping the agenda of fundamentalists. However, the reason for its comparative success seems to have been that after the initial shocks – which, after all, had begun as early as the seventeenth century – for a long time it was practised within a limited area. Worship remained largely untouched by it – and despite the wave of liturgical revision around the 1970s has continued to remain so; and so too did doctrine, in particular the key doctrines of Incarnation and Trinity. Those engaged in it who remained practising Christians could thus arrive at quite radical results while leaving large areas of faith and practice unquestioned. Perhaps the most striking figure in this respect was Rudolf Bultmann, whose technical work on the formation of the Synoptic Gospels and its implications for our knowledge (or lack of knowledge) of the historical Jesus made him notorious; despite all his questioning, in his theological approach he now looks more like a traditional Lutheran than anything else. Many Anglicans, too, seemed capable of combining radical views on the Bible with an acceptance of traditional Christian doctrine and liturgy.

Text and Tradition: Eating One's Cake and Having It

That was to change in 1966 when George Woods, Professor at King's College, London, followed by Maurice Wiles, pioneered what came to be known as 'doctrinal criticism'.

Before a premature death which prevented him putting his programme into action, George Woods had described the enterprise like this:

> Doctrinal criticism has its dangers to the Christian faith but I believe that, as in the nineteenth century the threat of biblical criticism was met by accepting its proper use, we ought in this century to meet the challenge of doctrinal criticism by a critical acceptance of its possibilities and legitimacy.[14]

It is worth noting the innocent throwaway phrase 'has its dangers to the Christian faith but . . .'!

Three years later, in 1969, Maurice Wiles, explained what this involved. The doctrinal critic

> is likely to conclude that the strong sense of Christ's absolute uniqueness as expressed in later doctrinal conviction is not something which emerges at all directly from the original teaching of Jesus himself – in so far as we are able to determine the precise content of that teaching with any confidence. Rather it is something which comes to consciousness within the life of the church which stemmed from him. Yet even here it does not seem to be the case that the radical nature of the conviction of the once-for-allness of Christ's work can be wholly accounted for as a necessary conclusion to be drawn from the new quality of life expressed in the early church. However profoundly transforming such an experience may have been, it could not logically be claimed to require as its cause a person or a happening of the radically unique kind which Christian doctrine has always affirmed. That would be to commit the same kind of fallacy as is generally agreed to be involved in any direct argument from the contingent and limited world to an absolute and finite God.[15]

In his book *The Making of Christian Doctrine*, published in 1967, he had already applied the approach of doctrinal criticism to a wide range of Christian doctrines, with illuminating and often devastating results, in particular showing up the weakness in the arguments used to construct them and the church-political pressures which were inextricably exerted in the process. The point was taken in some quarters, even in a report by the unexpurgated Church of England Doctrine Commission, and just as the Bible was coming to be read as stories, so too it was argued that Christian doctrine should be seen as stories – or even songs: Frances Young has bravely suggested that creeds are meant above all to be sung. But when the publication of *The Myth of God Incarnate*, to which Maurice Wiles and Frances Young were major contributors, brought the full glare of publicity to the doctrinal-critical approach, it became clear that the conclusions that would be drawn from doctrinal criticism would be very limited indeed – as Jews and Muslims hopeful of closer dialogue on a new basis found to their disappointment. Aspects of the approach of *The Myth* may have seeped through the churches by osmosis, so that later it could be claimed that most of the content of the book had been assimilated despite the objections raised to it, but it was not going to be allowed to undermine the official *status quo* – and this lack of willingness to pay the price of these insights was made all too clear when a sequel more directly concerned with inter-faith dialogue, *The Myth of Christian Uniqueness*, fell on virtually deaf ears.[16]

Schizophrenia

To say that this schizophrenia at the core of intellectual consideration of religious belief, particularly Jewish and Christian belief, cannot continue, would be foolish. History has shown, and present experience confirms, that all kinds of schizophrenia can continue – at least within the Christian churches. If it has been difficult to develop the approach of biblical criticism into doctrinal criticism (which realistically must so far be said to have failed in its aims), to extend doctrinal criticism into what might be called institutional criticism at present seems virtually impossible. Yet that seems to be precisely what is called for. Without some changes to mainstream Jewish and Christian thinking as it is usually expressed in public, the outlook for our divided world is bleak. If Christianity and Judaism, which have shared the same history for so long, and together faced the developments which have led to the formation of the modern world, cannot come closer together on the basis of the insights which these developments have brought, what faiths can?

I said earlier that if the consequences of the modern critical approach are ignored, a price has to be paid. That was no empty phrase. Elements of that price are evident enough. Growing militant fundamentalism: Christian against Jew against Muslim against Jew against Christian. The fuelling of political divisions by religious motivations. The increase of antisemitism and Christian nationalism in areas where these forces were once kept in check by Communist regimes. The further marginalization of religious belief and practice in the secularized Western world. If, as Hans Küng has urgently reminded us, there can be no peace among nations without peace among religions,[17] then one of the best places where those of different faiths can meet, and engage in dialogue, and grow together, is on the ground of that secular humanism (in the widest sense) which is represented by historical criticism (and in the wider world by the United Nations Universal Declaration of Human Rights, which belongs with this pattern of thinking). To pursue the argument further would take us into the question of what ethical foundations can be found today for the world in which we have to live together with as much human dignity as possible, and that is a question which no reading of the Bible, no endorsement of doctrine, no system of religious practices can fudge, ignore or set out to answer in an exclusivist way. Unfortunately, that is a further exploration of the implications of the critical approach which we cannot consider here.

We have come a long way from the point at which I began, but the coherence of the issues we have looked at on the way should be clear. Intimate dialogue cannot begin to solve all the problems that confront us, but it can at least begin to tackle some of them and see where that leads.

It should be plain from what I have said that I find the lack of inclination of Christians to tackle seriously the question of the status and foundation for Christian doctrine particularly painful, especially given the problems that the doctrines of both Trinity and Incarnation cause for Jews and Muslims. The need of the churches to think even a little here and to come clean on what they believe to be the foundations of their belief is all the more urgent as theological exploration has increasingly thrown up the tension between the supposedly biblical foundations of Christian doctrine (which are often virtually non-existent) and that doctrine itself.[18] Given the basic tenor of the critical work done on christology over the last decade, which has highlighted the gap between the New Testament evidence (let alone whatever Jesus may or may not have said and thought about himself) and the classical doctrine of the Incarnation,[19] how can the doctrine of the Incarnation be defended? And if the doctrine of the Incarnation is untenable, where does that leave the doctrine of the Trinity?[20] There is too much talk of Trinity and Incarnation as though they were established facts, instead of speculative human thought, and not enough reflection on what a new historical understanding demands as its consequences. It is harder, and indeed presumptuous, for a Christian to tell Jews what he thinks they should be doing, but among friends it is possible to speak more frankly than when writing for a totally unknown audience.

The schizophrenia to which I referred earlier does seem to me also to exist within Judaism, where I naturally find it more difficult to understand and assess than within my own tradition. As I indicated above, Jews recognize the importance of historical criticism; a Jew (albeit a renegade, Benedict Spinoza) stands right at the watershed between the ancient and the modern worlds in this respect, and in our own day Jews and Christians have joined together in the study of Jesus of Nazareth and the early church so closely that in many instances if one picked up a book of biblical or historical scholarship without the author's name on it would be hard to tell whether it had been written by a Jew or a Christian. I do not sense the existence of the same kind of shared interest in the origins of the people Israel, their patriarchs, the work of Moses and particularly his association with Torah, and the process by which they came to settle in the Promised Land. This is an area which has long fascinated me,[21] along with many other Christian theologians, and one in which the tension between critical findings and tradition is just as great as in the case of Jesus of Nazareth – with evidence just as hard to come by. How does Judaism reconcile its understanding of Torah with the circumstances in which Torah came into existence; how do Jews understand themselves in the light of the historical, rather than the traditional, way of looking at their origins? What if the exodus and the events on Sinai prove to be largely theological constructions from a very much later date, as many scholars think?[22] What if the historical picture of the early books of the Bible is essentially post-exilic? To ask these questions may prove just as traumatic as asking about the original Jesus of Nazareth, but in our modern world they cannot be ignored – nor can the possibility of the application of modern critical understanding to other areas of Jewish tradition and its consequences.

5. Is Historical Criticism Only a New Kind of Midrash?

JONATHAN MAGONET

There is a hasidic tale that is often quoted in Jewish-Christian dialogues. It is told that a hasidic rebbe overheard two peasants talking. One said, 'Ivan, do you love me?' To which Ivan replied, 'Of course I do.' 'Then do you know what causes me pain?' 'Of course not, how can I know that?' 'Then you do not really love me.'

The story is usually used by Jews complaining that their Christian partners in the dialogue have not really taken the trouble to understand the inner workings of the Jewish world, our suffering and the fears that drive us. In many cases it is a legitimate complaint, at least in an early stage of the dialogue, and one that has to be addressed. Unfortunately it is also sometimes used in a form of inverted triumphalism which excludes the Christian partner from even beginning to enter the Jewish world. It may even conceal a Jewish reluctance to address the issue of dialogue on the 'religious' level with which it is approached by the Christian. We are often more comfortable relating Jewish history, giving 'correct' information about Jewish tradition and ritual and culture (implying all too often a Jewish unity and uniformity in such areas that is far from the case), rather than taking the greater risk of exposing our inner religious questions. Sometimes this happens because the people invited to participate in 'dialogue' are themselves not particularly religious at all, being instead the Jewish 'academics' who happen to be authorities on the subject under discussion or the 'professionals' appropriate to the politics of the event. That in itself is not invalid, precisely because 'Judaism' and 'the Jewish people' embrace an enormous range of believers and non-believers, and it is legitimate to expose those seeking dialogue to this inner Jewish reality. But I can see how frustrating it must get when someone wishes to go deeper into what, for want of a better term, one may call Jewish 'spirituality', and finds no answering voice, or enters the dialogue ready to 'learn' on a personal level from Judaism, and does not find a reciprocal desire on the part of the Jewish partner, at least not in recognizable theological terms.

All of which is a preamble to a sort of apology to John Bowden. Because I have read his paper a number of times and must still confess that while I can feel in it an expression of pain at the inability of Christianity to address the doctrinal issues that he considers so central, I cannot quite understand the source or implication of that pain, particularly when he generalizes it to include Judaism. Perhaps the rest of this response is an attempt to enter the world he describes.

In beginning like this I am effectively endorsing his opening remarks about the value of a dialogue process that goes beyond formalism or abstract scientific curiosity. 'Dialogue' by implication means engagement on the human as well as the academic level and I hope to take up his implicit challenge.

I agree with his view that 'the great split *within* Judaism and *within* Christianity nowadays is between those who see Bible, doctrine, ministry, Torah or whatever as givens around which everything else revolves, and those who are so aware of the changes that have been brought by modern understanding, and particularly the historical consciousness that has arisen over the past two centuries . . . that they must give it a major place in their thinking about belief' (p. 54). Belonging as I do to the 'non-Orthodox' world, I must concur with his further suggestion that in this respect I may have more in common with Christian counterparts than with certain fellow-Jews. However, precisely because I am the product of almost two centuries of 'Reform' Judaism, which has lived throughout that time with 'higher criticism', its teeth have, to a large extent, become blunted by familiarity – though John might see this as evasion or selective inertia. Moreover, the Jewish relationship to the Hebrew Bible seems to be different to that of Christianity to its own textual tradition, so that our battle-lines with modernity are drawn elsewhere. However, before trying to examine where they might be, I feel obliged to comment on John's views on contemporary biblical scholarship.

Does correct doctrine matter?

I am not sure who in our group characterized biblical scholarship as 'dry, negative, pedantic and irrelevant'. I can sympathize with such a view in some ways, having from time to time been exposed to lecturers, and textbooks, that manage to reduce the drama of biblical scholarship to these levels. I have also been bewildered by Christian theologians, often German, trying to translate hypothetical, sub-divided, literary sources or schools into theological positions, based all too often on insufficient historical information and dubious political projections into the text. In fact, if inertia exists anywhere, it lies with some branches of contemporary biblical scholarship that still maintain an enormous superstructure derived from a critical theory whose specific criteria of analysis have long been challenged or disproved.

Some people can't help being boring, and some theories can't help being so reductionist that any 'theology' derived from them looks awfully dubious. So it is no wonder that many have embraced the new generation of literary analysts of the Bible, some of whom actually enjoy working with literature and have a style, not to say panache, of their own. But are their approaches and findings really just an aesthetic luxury? Are their scholarly credentials or hermeneutical principles less valid than those of previous generations? May it not be that they are actually applying the appropriate tools to the material at hand, uncovering the conventions of biblical writing against the background of its contemporary literature? For this approach, if any, is actually the necessary preliminary step before a more authentic historical evaluation of the biblical record can be undertaken.

I must acknowledge that I can only speak with any certainty about scholarship relating to the Hebrew Bible, and not that pertaining to the New Testament. But it may be that my views reflect a different attitude within Judaism to biblical exegesis. It is surely no accident that Jewish scholars have been among the pioneers of the newer forms of 'close-reading' of the text, precisely because these methods, in a suitably secular form, seem to leap across the centuries to link up with the classical tradition of rabbinical biblical exegesis – the *midrash*. They have much in common with an approach that treats the detail of the text with enormous seriousness – though understood then as the revealed word of God and today as the devoted expression of the author. Moreover it is important not to underestimate the deep seriousness of the midrashic tradition. Its apparent playfulness conceals a rabbinic awareness of the inner problems and contradictions of the texts before them. They were no less acute than nineteenth-century scholars in recognizing such matters; they merely adopted different hermeneutic principles in tackling them. And before we bow down to the god of 'scientific objectivity' it must be noted that Jewish tradition includes the great mediaeval scholars who created the scientific study of Hebrew grammar. Among their number is Abraham Ibn Ezra, who used comparative philology, with Arabic, in his biblical exegesis and a host of other scientific tools, including a critical evaluation of Jewish tradition and of the studies of contemporary scholars. He raised critical questions about the Mosaic authorship of the Pentateuch and identified two parts to the Book of Isaiah, and was a direct source of inspiration to Spinoza. This must be stressed, because alongside the rich 'midrashic' ('law and lore') component of Jewish Bible study there is a powerful strain of determined rationality, which often led its proponents, like Maimonides, into serious conflicts with their more conventionally pious co-religionists. In short, the Jewish exegetical tradition is rich in its pluralism of approach to the text, its acknowledgment of the validity of a multiplicity of interpretations, its willingness to challenge accepted and venerable traditions and authorities and its openness to living with contradiction and paradox.

Perhaps the clearest point of departure from Christian concern with correct doctrine is characterized by the Talmudic comment on the disagreements between the exegetical schools of Hillel and Shammai. A heavenly voice once intervened to resolve a particular problem with the statement that 'both these and these (opinions) are the words of the Living God. But the *halakhah* (the legal decision) goes according to the School of Hillel, because they tend to be more lenient in their rulings' (*Erubin 13b*). Here we see the point at which Jewish 'decision-making' is invoked – not in matters of doctrine, but with regard to practice, the concrete decision about some matter of legal obligation binding upon the community, be it in matters of daily life, liturgical practice or political action. We all have to cope with an invisible, unknowable God, and our human sanity requires that we find some concrete point upon which to anchor ourselves. If Christians (and here I must apologize for the vast generalizations that follow) do it by defining correct belief, Jews do it by defining correct action. So for the former, practice is 'open', but exegesis is circumscribed: for the latter, exegesis is wide open, but practice is controlled.

Which is not to say that things have not changed drastically within Judaism as a result of the Enlightenment and the assault on biblical authority that has arisen from 'higher criticism'. The fact that the Jewish world is divided into a variety of Orthodox and non-Orthodox religious movements as well as a whole host of 'secular' trends, ranging from Zionism through forms of socialism and humanism to indifference and assimilation, is ample testimony to a splitting of consciousness. But the intellectual questioning of Jewish 'doctrinal matters', if one can use such terminology, is not the ultimate determinative factor in Jewish 'identity', because we are always stumbling over the fact of Jewish peoplehood underpinning Jewish religiosity. There is also, in a strange way, a strong streak of 'religious secularism' built into Judaism, so that the *midrash* can have God say, 'I do not mind if they forsake Me, as long as they keep My Torah!' (*Proem Lamentations Rabbah* 2).[1] And that paradox can exist because so much of Jewish life is seen as the fulfilment of duties within the covenant family that have a sufficient weight of their own to survive even the breakdown of faith. Which leads to the classic paradox that a Jewish fundamentalist could be a rigorously observant Jew whose personal belief might be virtually non-existent. We operate a different sort of system from Christians, and the breakdown occurs in a different place.

So does it matter how Torah came into existence, or whether the Exodus or Sinai occurred as the Bible describes them or were actually post-exilic theological constructs, albeit reflecting ancient, possibly oral, traditions? The answer seems to be that it did matter desperately a century ago. Verifiable 'historical truth' was the criterion for a world engaged in an intellectual revolution. As much as the demythologization of the 'contents' of the Bible reflected a legitimate search for the 'historical truth' about the past, it also served a variety of anti-clerical, anti-doctrinal, humanist struggles with the 'authority' of the Bible. It mattered whether the event, as described in the Bible, actually took place or not, for if it could be shown that the text incorporated 'false history', then the religious traditions and powers that derived from it were equally suspect.

Today, when a materialist science is increasingly under question, and religious authority has been greatly undermined anyway, the newer approaches to the Bible are inevitably different. There is a greater recognition, at least in scholarly circles, that the materials we are dealing with in the Bible are the traditions about what took place, and that it is probably impossible to go behind them to what 'actually' did or did not happen. Nor is there sufficient material from within the Bible or from extra-biblical sources to fix with any degree of certainty how the tradition came about or was transmitted or edited into its final form. The nearest we can get to the nineteenth century's quest for 'historical truth' is to acknowledge that the Bible, in its multiplicity of volumes, is a composite of many sources and materials, that it is the result of a long tradition of reflection and editing, and that it represents the self-perception of Israelite society. But how that process came about, whose specific views the Bible represents and how to get behind the text to discover these things, seems ever more elusive. These are legitimate areas for speculation but no more than that. So we are increasingly forced back on the examination of what the text 'actually' says, though here, too, we must bear in mind the limitations that must be placed upon the interpretative exercise. The problem has shifted back again from 'history' to 'hermeneutics', but, unlike the 'pre-critical' period, to a hermeneutic with a more open-ended, and perhaps more self-conscious, set of criteria for evaluation. For example, this openness frees us from viewing the Hebrew Bible solely in terms of 'sacred history'. For this is a particular theological emphasis largely derived from a New Testament understanding of the 'Old' as being fulfilled in the 'New', a perception carried over into the academic world by generations of Christian (or ex-Christian) Bible scholars. As a new generation of literary scholars approach the text, they may be open to a far wider perception of the nature of the texts before them, which must inevitably have long-term consequences. Moreover we may increasingly come to recognize that the 'truth' of the Bible lies less in the 'facts' that it records and more, as Gabriel Josipovici suggests, and before him Martin Buber, in the dialogue to which it invites the reader.

From the Jewish point of view a number of factors may make it easier to cope with challenges raised by the classical historical criticism. Most obviously, whatever the challenges posed to the historicity of the Exodus or Sinai, we do not have to confront a problem like the divinity of Jesus. The 'fact' of the Exodus or the revelation at Sinai cannot be recovered, but the 'impact' of them upon Jewish self-understanding and historical consciousness, their mythic force and their shaping effect upon subsequent tradition, cannot be denied. And whatever else, they remain firmly within the sphere of human experience, even the act of revelation itself. Moreover the Hebrew Bible itself indicates, by showing the Sinai event from a variety of perspectives, notably that of the 'narrator' and the perception of the 'people', the 'human limitations' of any experience of God – the self-criticism of human abilities to experience and understand God is already built in. If post-biblical generations believed literally in Jonah's fish or Balaam's talking ass (Maimonides in the twelfth century demonstrated that the latter was only a visionary experience), that may not in any way have been the intention of the biblical authors themselves, and it is only in recent times that we have begun to recognize some of the clues they give to the reader to indicate this.

Biblical criticism can in a way help us 'purify' our reading of texts, but it still does not touch on the essential mystery that is common to all human creativity and the questions about revelation or inspiration at their heart. Whether God is present or not, either in the events themselves or in the process of their transmutation into texts, remains a matter of belief and conviction. How it comes about is ultimately unknowable. 'The sound of words you heard, but no image did you see!' (Deut.4.12).

If we examine where Jews stand today with regard to the inroads made by biblical criticism, we find a number of strategies for accommodating it. An ultra-Orthodoxy ignores the questions entirely. A middle-of-the-road Orthodoxy defends what it can and demands that faith cover the last irreducible components of Mosaic authorship of the Pentateuch. A variety of Liberal, Reform and Conservative movements take the scholarly issues as a given and live with a certain ambiguity and discomfort. They accept their value as part of their own battle to emancipate themselves from the authority of the tradition, or more accurately, the power of the Orthodox world of the last century. At the same time they have to struggle with defining their relationship to a tradition dominated by a concept of 'commandments', whose divine authority depends on a text whose authenticity they doubt. So they are forced to continue with a sort of 'as if' attitude to the tradition. They do so across a broad spectrum of belief and practice, ranging from almost total commitment to the classical tradition to the merest lip service. That is to say the question of revelation through the Bible is explored not in biblical textual analysis but in the theological, and political, struggle to define their relationship to the *halakhah* Jewish law.

Here too we enter a different set of problems, because *halakhah* derives ultimately not from the written revelation of Sinai, but from the oral tradition, also ascribed to Moses' experience at Sinai. And this is less susceptible to documentary analysis, precisely because the documents of an oral tradition, by definition, do not exist. Instead, the fact of there being an 'oral law' is the 'doctrinal basis' of Pharisaic and later Rabbinic Judaism. And since its authority has been shattered *de facto* in Jewish life since the Enlightenment, if not *de jure*, we are all, Orthodox and non-Orthodox alike, in the strange business of trying to hold it together in a sort of voluntary capacity. This is done, mostly, because of our fears about the breakdown of the 'unity' of the family. In effect, given the variety of non-Orthodox movements in Judaism, we have actually been living for the past century with the consequences of a Jewish equivalent of the 'doctrinal criticism' that John is advocating. But ultimately it is not a text that determines the historical authenticity or authority of the Exodus or Sinai; it is the evidence of our Jewish family tree and our collective memory.

It is surely no accident that the most radical Jewish re-thinking today about the Hebrew Bible comes not as a consequence of the 'higher criticism' but of the Shoah (see, for example, Emil Fackenheim's *The Jewish Bible After the Holocaust: A Re-reading*).[2] What moves Fackenheim is the impact, or rather the lack of an adequate impact, on Jewish and Christian religious consciousness of the Holocaust and the creation of the State of Israel, events which challenge all pre-war readings of scripture. A 'seamless' continuity of pre-war theological thinking is for him a scandal. But note that here too it is the impact of events affecting Jewish 'peoplehood' that is the prime mover towards a change of theology, not the other way round.

Do we share the heritage of the Enlightenment or of our faith communities?

At this point I must raise another aspect of John's paper where I find myself in disagreement, even on his own terms. For having asserted the importance of the personal encounter in dialogue, he seeks to limit it to those whose *a priori* like-mindedness effectively robs dialogue of its real potential for peacemaking, on the lines suggested by Hans Küng. Perhaps this is a reflection of the specific limitations of Jewish-Christian dialogue, where the agenda is too well-known and the immediate subjects for theological debate are presupposed. My own experience of dialogue with Muslims has opened up a far wider range of areas for exploration and has called upon a different set of 'qualifications' for participation. When a few of us first began such a dialogue some twenty years ago, it became evident that it was not on the basis of a shared 'secular humanism' that we could meet our Muslim partners, except in a very unconscious way. Rather it was a very explicit faith terminology, a willingness to share each others' prayer life, and a great deal of trust that God could bring us together despite the enormous barriers, religious and political, between us, through which any relationship at all could be established. Because in this case it was precisely with 'fundamentalists', and only with them, that a dialogue was available. Which meant for the 'liberal' Jewish participants an enormous leap of imagination and understanding to enter a world that, in our home territory of Judaism, we would have entered with considerable discomfort – if allowed in at all on such terms. And this proved of inestimable value, in part because of the integrity, faith and generosity of spirit of those we met, and in part because it drew out of us a greater degree of trust in precisely those elements in Jewish tradition, notably faith and prayer, which sit most uneasily on a liberal consciousness. Since these were the only people we could meet, we had to stretch our spiritual resources for such an encounter, and learnt that the way to make our faith grow was by exercising it in this way, taking it to where we had never intended. Moreover, we gained a greater degree of understanding of the sacrifices, invisible to us initially, made by our dialogue partners in risking the meeting with us. There is a sort of cultural snobbishness that expects that the other, in entering a dialogue with us, make compromises on our terms and in ways that we recognize: 'Why can't they just accept our food in the spirit of friendship!?' 'Why must we always yield to the fundamentalists?' It takes a long time before we are able to recognize and value what they experience themselves as having to risk or give up in meeting with us. Of course, this is no more than what we Jews tend to ask of Christians when they approach us – so it was particularly healthy to have to reciprocate when approaching the world of Islam.

The point of these observations is to question one of John's basic assumptions. He argues that 'one of the best places where those of different faiths can meet, and engage in dialogue, and grow together, is on the ground of that secular humanism (in the widest sense) which is represented by historical criticism (and in the wider world by the United Nations Universal Declaration of Human Rights, which belongs with this pattern of thinking)' (p. 59). However, I find this entirely too narrow a focus and indeed one that risks reducing dialogue to the 'abstract and clinical' level that John so rightly condemns. Meeting our mirror images in a shared humanistic environment is comforting but no less an evasion, in terms of what dialogue can potentially offer, than finding a variety of ways of living with the discomfort produced by 'higher criticism'. It is surely the acknowledgment of the differences of the other, and nevertheless making the imaginative leap to try, in however limited a way, to enter his or her world, that is the essence of dialogue. And if, even at some remove, the aim of the exercise is 'peace', then the same applies as in any conflict situation – we have to make peace with the one who is our actual 'opponent', not the ones we would like to be our opponent, and that means accepting them in their otherness and broadening our own parameters of understanding.

There may be a lesson from this in terms of John's concern with a 'conservatism' within the church. One of the paradoxes of dialogue on this level is that 'orthodox' and 'liberals' who meet across faith boundaries, out of necessity, may ultimately learn how to tolerate and even enjoy their 'orthodox' or 'liberal' counterparts within their own community. Some of the self-righteous anger on both sides may become diffused because they have stood, if only for a little while, in the equivalent of the other's shoes, and if there is a degree of affection generated in the interfaith relationships, it may ultimately spill over into the intra-faith situation.

At the bottom line, any faith assumption is an irrational act, and all our religious systems are merely methods of rationalizing it – whether this is done at the level of scriptural analysis, covenantal patterns of behaviour or abstract theology. Therefore an assault on the system, which is essential as a means of its regular self-purification, is nevertheless limited by the extent of our own personal inner security, trust and belief. We may and must criticize our religious system in the name of justice without limits, because that is one of the essential tasks of at least our monotheistic religions. But an assault that challenges some ultimate belief in the name of historical objectivity is potentially self-defeating. This is partly the case because our tools of historical analysis are themselves fallible – and it would be absurd to make truth claims for them as great as the truth claims of the system we are questioning. But on another level we are actually squabbling about where we draw the line of rationality over that initial 'leap of faith', that of our community or our own personal one. And our ability to be free to be critical seems to depend, paradoxically, on the depth and security of our faith in the first place, on the degree to which this faith is backed by some sort of religious experience, and how far we have worked on nourishing and refining and indeed challenging it. This becomes particularly crucial if 'faith' is the primary operating criterion in our religious identity, as it would seem to be for Christianity. Without a sense of peoplehood to fall back on, as offering another parameter of belonging to a particular faith community, I can well imagine the threat posed by a challenge to what must ultimately be our own arbitrary decision about where to limit enquiry, and the frustration of those who would wish to push the boundaries outward. But there may also be a level of wisdom in knowing how far one can go without risking the whole edifice, provided that there is a commitment to re-examining matters at a later date. (It is one of the sources of Jewish pride, and hence continual renewal, that the minority view in Talmudic debates was preserved alongside the majority decision, so that the matter could always be reopened and the legitimacy of alternative views, and of their representatives, acknowledged.) In these terms perhaps the task of an inner Christian dialogue would be in helping each other to increase trust and security on a variety of levels, particularly spiritual, so that the intellectual challenges can be more readily confronted and absorbed. But that requires a far-reaching programme of mutual strengthening and education, and one not limited to the intellect alone.

I am reminded of Soloviev's *The Antichrist*, which still seems a remarkable paradigm of the religious traps into which our various traditions can fall.[3] As I recall it, the 'antichrist', in the guise of a messianic saviour, gains power in the world. In order to keep the churches quiet, he offers each of them what they most desire. Thus the Pope is offered a huge building in which to keep the entire bureaucracy of the Catholic church. The Russian Orthodox representative is offered a museum of antiquities in which to preserve every conceivable religious relic. The Protestants, in the person of a professor of theology, are offered a university in which they can teach theology with total academic freedom, using the most modern critical tools. I cannot recall if the Jews were offered anything, but they were among the first to challenge the authority of this would-be Messiah on discovering that he had not been circumcised! (It is right that the Jews would have made a fuss on that level of detail!)

Perhaps Soloviev saw here the negative expression of three great values enshrined in the respective churches: community, tradition and reason. Each have their traps, but each emphasizes something different and must be challenged in those specific terms. The wealth of our respective religious traditions has to be a constant reminder that we are strong, and vulnerable, in quite different ways. If Western Christianity is sensitive about the enterprise of biblical criticism and thus finds ways of avoiding the more unpalatable conclusions, then it may well be right to challenge that evasion, provided one makes a serious attempt to address the underlying fear itself and offer a relevant support, particularly if one is certain of the benefits that will arise from the purification such challenges may bring. But if that support is not on offer as well, then the intellectual exercise alone may do as much harm as it does good.

I would nevertheless still wish to argue that the situation for Judaism is different, not only because of the 'peoplehood' factor, but also because Judaism has had an almost unbroken tradition of biblical exegesis. Indeed it has been through the medium of biblical exegesis that we have responded to intellectual challenges posed throughout the centuries, living as we have under Christianity and Islam and having to respond to both. The question for us today seems to be whether 'higher criticism' will ultimately be perceived (and it may take a few more centuries to find out) as a radically different challenge that really does undermine the authority of the Jewish scriptures – or will prove instead to be a different kind of culturally determined 'midrash', challenging in its implications, leading to some major reassessments and realignments within the tradition, but not ultimately fatal. At this moment we do not really know. But if Judaism is to continue to speak from a religious centre, interfaith dialogue may be one of the essential resources that helps us find our way.

6. Myth and Morality

HYAM MACCOBY

I am grateful to John Bowden for raising a very important issue in Jewish-Christian relations. He points out that Christianity and Judaism share a common dilemma, the confrontation with modern scientific criticism, both textual and sociological. Textual criticism has impaired the authority of both Christian and Jewish sacred writings, by showing their human origin (with all this entails in the way of redaction of varied sources, ideological slanting and pseudepigraphy). Sociology has shown how doctrines regarded as primitive and divinely inspired have actually developed gradually through the impact of social forces. John believes that this common dilemma, requiring re-interpretation of the meaning of faith and radical revision of doctrines, should bring Christianity and Judaism together. The internal rift, he argues, between those in each religion who seek to cope with the new critical insights and those who ignore them, precludes any simple view of a unitary Christianity combating a unitary Judaism.

John finds to his surprise, however, that neither Christians nor Jews, even when fully cognizant of modern criticism, seem to be sufficiently aware of the seriousness of the crisis. Christians, on the one hand, avoid any fundamental reconsideration of the doctrines of the Incarnation and the Trinity, despite knowledge of the human processes by which these doctrines were introduced and their absence in the earliest sources. On the other hand, John asks why Jews do not find a challenge in critical views of Moses and the Exodus, which could be just as traumatic, he suggests, as questions about the history and sociology of christology for Christians. A common awareness of crisis, which might have been a powerful force for mutual sympathy, has been dissipated by unwillingness to face unpleasant truths.

I suggest, however, that the matter is rather more complicated than this. The time has long passed when evidence of human authorship of scriptural writings and doubts about their literal historical truth were traumatic for religious believers. Ruskin or Matthew Arnold may have suffered such trauma, and many nineteenth-century Jews too felt the agony of loss of faith because of Wellhausian source criticism of the Pentateuch or textual research into the books of Samuel. Many Jews who became converted to Communism or other atheistic faiths could trace their disillusion with Judaism to this origin. Those who remained believers (apart from simple-minded fundamentalists who retained mediaeval attitudes) did so by redefining faith. Sociology, which John cites as a dissolver of faith, also acted as its restorer, when it became clear (through the work of Durkheim and others) that all societies are built on some religious foundation-myth that acts with symbolic force in organizing all phases of communal life and thus has a 'truth' more profound than fact. Christian and Jewish believers could be redefined as those attached respectively to the Christian and Jewish myths.

Perhaps the most articulate exponent of this transition is Rudolf Bultmann, whom John cites as someone in whom knowledge of criticism failed to produce radical theological change. But Bultmann was precisely concerned with presenting a mode of faith that was a response to criticism. He destroyed the historical Jesus ruthlessly by critical means, only to assert that faith was not to be based on the historical Jesus but on the mythical Christ. His programme of 'demythologization' was meant not to denigrate myth but to enthrone it as the subject-matter of theological exegesis, which was to consist of the decoding of the myth in modern terms. This meant indeed that traditional christology was reinstated as immune to the critical approach. But this was the end-result of criticism itself, not a lapse from it.

John rightly does not like this, because it amounts to the restoration of fundamentalist belief, now based not on the inerrancy of scripture but on the rightness and symbolic truth of the myth conveyed by scripture under the guise of telling a historical story. What John wants is to criticize the myth itself, and he says that he wants to do so (in the form of 'doctrinal criticism') on the basis of textual and sociological criticism that shows that the myth was a slow accretion rather than an explosive revelation. To this Bultmann would reply that the way the myth developed is irrelevant: we are not concerned with historical fact but with symbolic value; the final flowering of a rose is not invalidated by itemizing the stages by which it developed.

A moral criticism of myth

I would put the matter in the following way. Textual or sociological criticism does not in itself invalidate a myth; but it does open the way to such invalidation. Once a myth loses its support in supposedly inerrant texts, it becomes open to analysis; but such analysis is now no longer itself textual or sociological, but moral. Once we move from textual or sociological criticism to 'doctrinal criticism', we enter a new dimension. We are no longer asking, 'What is the myth's authority? Does it have incontestable truth because of its divine origin?' Instead we are asking, 'Is this a good or a bad myth?' Alternatively, 'Does this myth, when interpreted for the modern world by demythologization, convey the highest moral and spiritual truth? Or does it, on the contrary, judged by its moral implications and its historical fruits, convey a flawed message?'

Bultmann himself never really asks this question. He assumes that once the Christian myth has been detached from textual and sociological considerations, it shines forth as the highest expression of symbolic thought. A similar attitude animates the Jungian general rehabilitation of myth, popularized by writers such as Joseph Campbell, usually with the conclusion that Christianity forms the apex of mythological thinking.

It was the great merit of *The Myth of God Incarnate*, to which John rightly points as a watershed, that it did not satisfy itself with textual or sociological criticism of the Christian myth of the Incarnation, but went on to criticize it on moral grounds. The deification of Jesus was held responsible for the political imperialism associated with the history of Christendom. Also, the claim that Christ was the unique giver of salvation, entailed by his divinity, was shown to have led to the annihilation or oppression of rival faiths and 'heresies'. The demonstration that the formulation of the doctrine of the Incarnation was a gradual process was not the chief ground of criticism: rather it aimed at showing that (a) the doctrine of the divinity of Jesus was historically vulnerable, and (b) an alternative doctrine of the non-divinity of Jesus was available in the sources and indeed had earlier authority. Thus the way was open to criticism of the doctrine of the Incarnation on moral grounds without destroying the foundations of Christian faith.

My own reservation about *The Myth of God Incarnate* is that it did not state the moral case against the Incarnation strongly enough, since the issue of Christian antisemitism was not raised, except incidentally as part of the argument about intolerance. Antisemitism, however, is a special case, springing directly out of the Christian myth of divinity, rather than being a mere off-shoot of the claim to uniqueness. The Jews have an important role among the *dramatis personae* of the myth, being cast as the killers of the sacrificed God. If Jesus had never been deified, the Jews would, at most, have played the same role in the Christian imagination as the Athenians responsible for the death of Socrates. As it was, the Jews were demonized as the predestined slayers of God. Such a role could only be played by a people who were the earthly representatives of Satan, Jesus' cosmic antagonist. The alleged crime of the Jews was essential to the scenario of salvation; but this did not absolve them, any more than Judas Iscariot, from detestation.

Moral criticism of the Jewish myth cannot be sustained

Given the above reformulation of the impact of criticism on Christian belief, the question may now be asked (following John), 'What impact should criticism have on Jewish belief?' If the Jewish myth no longer has the authority of inerrant scripture, is it now vulnerable to moral criticism? The basic Jewish myth is that of the Exodus from Egypt, the giving of the Torah in the desert, and the conquest of the Promised Land. Do the moral fruits of this myth require a radical 'doctrinal criticism' such as was offered against the doctrine of the Incarnation by *The Myth of God Incarnate*? Does the religious civilization built upon this myth contain serious flaws traceable to the moral effects of the myth itself, in the way suggested by Christian civilization?

Certainly such moral criticism of the Jewish myth has been offered often enough in the past. A recent book, Dan Jacobson's *The Story of the Stories*,[1] might perhaps be offered as a Jewish parallel to *The Myth of God Incarnate*, since it provides moral criticism by a Jew of the basic Jewish myth. Jacobson's thesis is that the chief purpose of the Exodus myth was to emphasize the chosenness of the Israelites as a dominant people. The conviction of chosenness, he argues, is morally questionable, since it promotes intolerance and even genocide. The historical fruits of the myth of chosenness were the Boer conviction of white supremacy and the Nazi theory of Aryan superiority. While Jacobson does see some good moral fruits of the doctrine of chosenness, he thinks that they are heavily out-weighed by the bad.

Jacobson's criticism, in my view, is based on total misunderstanding of the Jewish myth. The Israelites were not chosen because of their innate superiority, as in racist theory. On the contrary, it is emphasized that they were the lowest of slaves, and required a hard education to make them even remotely worthy of their mission. They were chosen not because of what they *were*, but because of what they were called upon to do. Consequently, the Bible record is all about their failings and backslidings. One cannot imagine any racist record outlining the failings of, say, the Aryan race; on the contrary, the propaganda is devoted to the race's superior virtue, beauty and attainments.

Thus the concept of chosenness in Judaism is at the opposite pole to its caricatures in racist doctrine. Further, the chosenness of Israel did not entail a programme of conquest to convert the world. The conquest of the

Promised Land was necessary to set up the project outlined in the Torah, but the Israelites and their leaders, the prophets, were far too unsure of their own ability to implement this programme themselves to be much concerned about propagating it abroad (though they accepted proselytes who came to them such as Naaman and Ruth). Thus Christians conquering South America, or Boers South Africa, who cited the invading Israelites as their model were grotesquely beside the point: there was no valid analogy between attacks on aborigines by developed civilizations with a secure home base and an invasion by landless escaped slaves against entrenched heavily-armed slave-states in the hope of setting up a revolutionary free society.[2]

It is unjust, therefore, to see the moral fruits of the Exodus myth as the Christian and Muslim attempts at world-conquest, much less the Nazi theories of the chosen race. On the contrary, the moral fruits of the Exodus are to be seen in movements of liberation, such as the English Puritan Revolution and the American Revolution. This is the thesis of Michael Walzer's excellent book, *Exodus and Revolution*,[3] which is not content with stating a general thesis, but substantiates it by citing the statements, speeches and even private diaries of the apostles of liberation in England and America, showing how the metaphors of the Israelite Exodus, tribulations and back-slidings in the desert, and conquest of the Promised Land featured prominently in their thoughts.

But does the Jewish claim to chosenness entail a doctrine of uniqueness similar to that conferred on Christianity by the Incarnation? I rather suspect that this is what is in John's mind when he suggests parallel policies of jettisoning of doctrines. If both religions can surrender their special claims, they can turn to each other as comrades and embark on true pluralism.

I am afraid, however, that, as far as Judaism is concerned, I cannot see any true parallel. Judaism has never claimed that it is the unique road to salvation, nor does the story of the Exodus imply any such claim. If the Israelites were singled out for a special vocation, that does not imply any bar to salvation for other peoples. The most that the Jews have claimed is that, as the pioneers of monotheism (singled out for this role not by their own merit or talents but by the stupendous event of the Exodus), they are entitled to a special respect. But they never thought that their special rule of holiness had to be practised by other peoples to gain salvation, any more than, say, the Dominicans regard non-Dominican Catholics as damned. If the Jews wish to take upon themselves special responsibilities, why should others feel so diminished that they should demand ordinariness for the Jews as a condition of ecumenism? Such an idea, if carried to its logical conclusion, would demand that all the civilizations or even individuals that have contributed something special to world culture should renounce their strivings in the interests of a dead-level mediocrity. The renunciation of uniqueness surely cannot mean this.

Yet a renunciation of Christianity's traditional claims to uniqueness is undoubtedly required if ecumenism is to mean anything. This has been very different from a mere claim to a special vocation. The doctrine of the Incarnation means that God himself died on the cross, and this can only be for the sake of mankind as a whole for whom the crucifixion provides the only hope of salvation. Thus Christianity's 'universalism', on which it has so often prided itself as against Judaism's 'particularism', is precisely what stands in the way of ecumenism. Is there perhaps some way of interpreting the Incarnation that would allow the validity of other faiths for salvation? This is the question that is occupying many Christian minds today. John and others, however, think that the only solution for Christians is to jettison the doctrine of the Incarnation, which, they argue, has no great claim on their loyalty, since it is not 'primitive', but arose gradually for largely political or sociological reasons. I myself find their case totally convincing, and as a Jew I hope that it will prevail, though as John says, the reaction to it has not been encouraging, despite an initial period of apparent receptiveness.

But is it not Jewish doctrine that God himself gave the Torah on Sinai, and is this not a parallel to the Christian claim that God himself died on the cross, entailing the same claim to uniqueness? Here we must invoke a number of Jewish beliefs, which have given offence in the past but now look like a blueprint for ecumenism: that the Torah was given only to the Jews (who include, of course, converts); that the Gentiles have their own revelation covenant, the Noachide dispensation, by which they may achieve salvation without conversion to Judaism or practice of the Torah; that Judaism is a universal belief, but not a universal church; that the Jews welcome all monotheistic faiths, provided only that they do not base their authority on a claim to have transcended Judaism and rendered it obsolete (with the corollary that the Jews are wicked not to have acknowledged their own obsolescence); that, on the contrary, the Jews have a special claim to respect as the pioneers of monotheism.

Thus the situation seems to me much more one-sided than John suggests. Christianity has a long way to go to achieve true ecumenism, while Judaism has achieved it long ago, since ecumenism is actually built into the basic myth of the Exodus, which concerns the spiritual and physical liberation of a specific people. The rest of mankind may look to the Jewish experiment for guidance and inspiration, but are expected by Jews to engage in their own spiritual adventures. The story of the Exodus is set, certainly, in a universal background (otherwise the Bible would have started with

Abraham or Moses, not with Adam), but the Jews form only one set of players in the universal game.

Thus the future of ecumenical relations between Christians and Jews depends on a significant shift in thinking by Christians. It is not a question of Jews being prepared to shed doctrines *pari passu* with Christians, thus becoming comrades in doctrinal bereavement, as John seems to suggest.[4]

The question that now interests me is how far Jews should be prepared to help Christians in their dilemma. John suggests this question by his concern for a dialogue that is not confined to mutual self-explanation but enters into the difficulties experienced by the other side. I heartily endorse this conception of dialogue. It means, in the case of the struggle towards true ecumenism, that Jews must declare their support for Christian thinkers such as John Bowden, George Woods, Maurice Wiles and John Hick, who wish to jettison the main obstacle to Christian-Jewish reapproachment, namely the doctrine of the Incarnation.

But it must be acknowledged that this matter involves far more than the issue of ecumenism. To jettison the Incarnation would imply, for most people, a great difference in religious philosophy: a change from other-worldly hopes of immortality to a this-worldly religious humanism similar to that of Judaism. Should Jews intervene in internal Christian conflict in a matter of such wide-ranging significance?

Many Jews would certainly feel a great reluctance to do so, especially in the light of their own experience of Christian intervention in Jewish theology (the banning or censorship of the Talmud, for example). Yet are we Jews to turn away from these people just when they need us, and when there is a growing body of Christians themselves who are struggling to divest themselves of the doctrine of the Incarnation on philosophical, historical and moral grounds? Having for millennia stood out against religious anti-humanism and exclusive claims of salvation, are we to adopt a neutral stance just when there is some hope of putting our view to an increasingly sympathetic Christian audience?

I welcome and applaud John Bowden's courageous quest, even though I do not feel able to share in it on quite the same terms that he suggests.

Part Three
Shoah, Suffering and Theodicy

7. The Power of Suffering Love

MARCUS BRAYBROOKE

Can the church be redeemed?

> Am I a fool to be an active member of a church that proclaims love as its motivating energy when historically . . . ?[1]

The question which the American Harry James Cargas asks himself in his *Shadows of Auschwitz* is likely to haunt any Christian who acknowledges the depth of Christian complicity in the Shoah. Eleven million people were murdered by the Nazis. Six million of them were Jews. One million of the Jews were children. They were murdered in the heartland of Christian Europe. Those who harried the Jews and most of the guards and those who administered the policy of death were baptized Christians. Even Hitler, a baptized Catholic, was never excommunicated.

Nazism was anti-Christian, but it is clear that it was only able to take root in Germany because of centuries of Christian anti-Jewish teaching. In other parts of Europe, many people colluded with the Nazis and only a few actively resisted their persecution of the Jews.

The Shoah, although the most horrific attack on the Jews, was not an isolated event. The history of Christian Europe is marred by persecution, massacre and pogrom.

Increasingly, Christians are acknowledging that much of their teaching over the centuries has been false. It was wrong to blame the Jews for the death of Jesus ('deicide'). The New Testament picture of the Pharisees is a caricature. The church has not replaced the Jews as 'the people of God'. All this is being recognized in official statements of the churches, even if it is still not widely known by members of those churches.[2]

Yet even if the churches rid themselves of overt anti-Judaism – and Jewish friends may think there is still a long way to go – will this cure the sickness? I fear there is a triumphalism close to the centre of much Christian preaching which sees the other as a threat, an opponent of God, to be converted, suppressed or even destroyed. I have been moved by feminist theologians who have seen the oppression of the Jews and the oppression of women as both being an expression of this triumphalism. People of other faiths and people not of European origin have suffered too at the hands of Christian Europeans. Indeed they continue to suffer economic exploitation.[3]

I was made very aware of this oppression recently at a conference in Costa Rica. Memories of the genocide that accompanied the Spanish conquest and the 'Christian evangelization of the continent' are still fresh in the minds of the indigenous people. They continue to suffer discrimination and dispossession of their land. Their story is echoed by the aboriginals of Australasia.

The church in many centuries and in many places – not quite 'everywhere and always' – has been an oppressive and persecuting body. Is it just that the church has failed to check human sinfulness and that Christianity has never been tried? Is it that the church has colluded with the abuse of power? I suspect the latter is true, and that too often Christians have ascribed despotic power to God and then behaved in the image of this god. By contrast, the message and death of Jesus speaks of the suffering love of God. In my view, the abuse of power by the church and by Christian nations in their imperialism reflects a far-reaching misunderstanding of the nature of God's power as shown by Jesus.

Am I a fool to be an active member of a church that proclaims love as its motivating energy when historically . . . ?

Why our picture of God matters

I believe that our picture of ultimate reality, whether or not thought out, profoundly affects our outlook and behaviour. Yet, today there is often an impatience with theology. For example, the suffragan Bishop of Brixworth, Paul Barber, recently objected to his fellow bishops' persistent use of the word 'theologically'. He was objecting to jargon and went on to insist upon the importance of theology. But to many, to say that something is theological is as bad as to say that it is academic. It is, by implication abstruse and irrelevant.[4]

On the contrary, I have become increasingly aware that our picture of God and our vision of ultimate reality has a profound effect on our attitudes and behaviour. If we think of God as a 'great traffic warden in the skies', we shall always be looking over our shoulder, and our attitude to wrong-doers will be punitive. For example, writing during the Gulf War, Tony Higton, an outspoken conservative evangelical Anglican clergyman, said,

'I suspect some of the anti-war idealism is related to the widespread modern reaction against discipline and punishment.' His emphasis on punishment is based on his view of the way in which God deals with sinful men. In his book, *What is the New Age?*, he writes, 'Without a terrible death-penalty (inflicted on Christ) God's just law could not be satisfied and mankind saved.'[5] If, however, we picture God as a mother comforting us in our sorrow, our hope will be that any punishment is remedial. The 'universalist' who believes that in the end all people will be saved will trust that the most hardened criminal can be changed. Those who believe in hell-fire are likely to accept that some wrongdoers must be destroyed. In wartime, people often assume that God is on their side, but if we picture a God who loves people of all religions equally, then God's concern is peace and justice for all.

Often the consequences that flow from our picture of God are unrecognized and unacknowledged. My picture of God has changed over the years. Yet I have tried to combine this emerging picture with old-established doctrinal positions and a traditional structure of faith – not to mention liturgical formulae – which are based on suppositions that I no longer share. I am typical of those whom John Bowden describes as attempting to eat their cake and have it (p. 55).

My picture of God as suffering love has changed my attitude to war and peace and to penal policy, as well as purifying my understanding of prayer and giving me a terrifying sense of our human responsibility for the future. The Shoah makes clear the evil consequences that flow from a false picture of God. The substitutes put in the place of the True God legitimize greed, cruelty and destruction. As Hugo Gryn, a leading British rabbi and Shoah survivor has said, Auschwitz is about man and his idols, about abominable things set up in the place of God.[6]

'There is no God to whom I could pray with my back turned toward Auschwitz'

The question, then, is not just about the credibility of the church. It becomes one about the nature of God. This has occupied many Jewish thinkers since the Shoah and those Christian theologians – too few – who struggle with the same question know their debt to these Jewish writers.[7]

Often the question is treated as if it were the traditional question of theodicy. It has been said that the Shoah does not ask any new questions, but puts them more sharply than ever before. I sense, however, that the radical German theologian Dorothee Sölle is right when she suggests that the question of theodicy is a false question. It starts with the assumption that God is omnipotent, intelligible and loving. The theologian then appears as counsel for the defence to try to argue, despite the evidence, that God indeed has these qualities. Dorothee Sölle suggests that 'the religious question of suffering is no longer the one so often heard: how can God permit that?, but a more difficult one, which first has to be studied: how does our pain become God's pain and how does God's pain appear in our pain?'[8]

The question arises from the experience in the midst of deep suffering of a presence that we sense to be divine. Dorothee Sölle writes that:

It is our task to transform 'wordly grief' into the pain of God, and with the pain of God I, who live after the Jewish holocaust and who in recent years have used my strength in the framework of the peace movement against the atomic holocaust, I am undergoing a singular experience. The pain is not soothed, calmed or falsified, but it brings nevertheless a deep joy. It is as if my hands were touching the power of life, which is also in pain, the pain which indeed, biologically, is life's protest against illness and death and which indeed hurts us for the sake of life. I am not talking of God as an automatic machine which sends peace after pain and rain after sun. I see the sun in the rain. I do not wish to seek the power without the pain, for that would mean separating myself from God and betraying God's pain. 'The people who walked in darkness have seen a great light; those who dwelt in a land of deep darkness, on them has light shined' (Isaiah 9.1). From where does such a precept come, if not from the pain of God! How can we see darkness and light together if not in Him who comprises both!

What I am trying to say sounds mystical, but you all know it already and have often heard it before: it is hidden in Johannes Brahms' piano concerto in D minor, because great music deals with God's pain and plunges into us.[9]

This passage has helped me to clarify what I am trying to say. It links to the insight of mystics of several traditions and to the Hindu perception that God is both life-giver and destroyer, that the divine is present in life and death, in joy and sorrow.

In a small way, the closer I have come to the suffering of others, the more strongly I have sensed the divine pity. In trying to care for the destitute in India, in sitting with a parent whose daughter had just been murdered, in listening to a friend whose family was exterminated at Belsen, in speaking with those whose loved ones have been crushed in a torture cell in Latin America, I have sensed that God was there. Perhaps most vividly, once as I left the bedside of a parishioner who was dying of an acutely painful cancer, I felt utterly speechless and unable to offer words of comfort and then had an overwhelming feeling of God's presence. Others, such as witnesses to faith in the camps, have known that God is with them at the eye of the storm.

If such experiences are our starting point, then the traditional questions of theodicy may seem artificial, because they do not speak of a God known at such moments. The experience, as Dorothee Sölle puts it, is of God as our mother 'who cries about what we do to each other and about what we brothers and sisters do to animals and plants'.[10]

Dr Chung Hyun-Kyung, in her startling address to the World Council of Churches Canberra Assembly, said, 'I rely on the compassionate God who weeps with us for life in the midst of the cruel destruction of life'.[11] The experience of God's presence with us in pain changes our picture of God and also reshapes our response to God.

God's power is the power of suffering love

The picture of God as suffering love has become increasingly important to me. As it has done so, my understanding of other aspects of faith has been changed. I begin to see that to emphasize God's suffering love implies rejecting traditional descriptions of God as omnipotent, impassible and omniscient. It follows that prayer does not change God, but us. Further, this picture of God suggests that the future is in our hands and, if we are to shape a more just and peaceful world, we should imitate God's way of suffering love.

I am conscious that the concept has become more central for me as I have pondered the implications of the Shoah. The Shoah hangs over all Christian-Jewish dialogue 'as a dark, powerful and accusing cloud'.[12] A prerequisite for honest conversation is acknowledgment by Christian participants of their churches' share of responsibility for Jewish suffering. Even then, there is a proper hesitancy about speaking of a suffering that nobody who was not there can comprehend. There is a hesitancy, too, about theologizing as a Christian about what was primarily a Jewish tragedy of appalling dimension and of appearing to apply to it ways of thinking drawn from the Christian tradition.[13] Yet, the horror of the Holocaust challenges all faith in God's goodness. I cannot forget that horror when I speak of God or speak to God. Inevitably, too, my thinking is moulded by the Christian tradition that has shaped me.

In one sense this is nothing new. Several passages in the Bible affirm that God is with us in our sufferings (Ps. 23.4; Ps. 139). The crucifixion has suggested to Christians God's deep involvement in human pain. There is a saying in the Talmud that 'when God remembers his children who dwell in misery among the nations of the world, he causes two tears to fall into the ocean and the sound is heard from one end of the world to the other' (Babylonian Talmud, Tractate Berachot, 29a).

Yet the comfort of God's presence with the sufferer is often combined with a continuing belief in God's majesty or sovereign power. For some this belief was shattered by the First World War. For those who lived through it, the war was 'like a band of scorched earth dividing' pre-war and post-war reality. The war 'created a physical as well as a psychological gulf between two epochs'.[14] G. Studdert-Kennedy, for example, writing after the First World War, strongly rejected old pictures of God's power. 'We can no longer,' he said, 'interpret ultimate reality in the terms of absolute monarchy if we are to reach the hearts of men.'[15]

James Parkes, who was to become a pioneer of a new Christian understanding of Judaism, felt that the suicidal war demanded a new way of thinking about religion and politics.[16]

The Shoah was even more shattering, despite the fact that many Christian theologians have carried on their business as before.[17] The uniqueness of the Holocaust makes it more than 'one more instance of human cruelty'.[18] The reality of evil has always been a challenge to belief in a God of love, but for many the Shoah shattered old pictures. 'Nothing before,' writes Arthur A. Cohen, 'achieves more than a gloss of the enormity.'[19]

In the shadow of the Shoah, only a suffering God is credible to me. A God who could have acted and did not is not worthy of worship. I recognize that my picture of God as suffering love is shaped by an understanding of the death of Jesus which has come to me through some of the Christian tradition. Jesus accepted cruelty and mockery without answering bitterness. Words of Isaiah were soon used to describe his death: 'He was afflicted, he submitted to be struck down and did not open his mouth' (Isa. 53.7). The object of hatred, there was no hatred in him. He prayed for those who caused his death. The hope is that such vulnerability and acceptance of enmity eventually drains it of its power. Hatred which is absorbed without response loses its venom.

Love, which through suffering absorbs evil and is completely vulnerable, is of its very nature indestructible. Such love cannot be defeated by evil and death, whereas enmity eventually exhausts itself. The resurrection of Jesus, beyond questions about what happened, is the recognition of the invincible character of self-giving love.[20] In such love, I believe that the deepest meaning of life is revealed. The cross, therefore, for me discloses the nature of God and the way to life.

The glory of the cross

Such an understanding of the cross draws upon the Fourth Gospel. The Fourth Evangelist suggests that the self-giving death of Jesus on the cross was also the moment when God's glory was revealed. In John 12, when some Greeks ask to see Jesus, he replies, 'The hour has come for the Son of Man to be glorified. In truth, in very truth I tell you, a grain of wheat remains a solitary grain unless it falls into the ground and dies, but if it dies it bears a rich harvest' (John 12.23–24). Then, in a passage which echoes the Synoptic Gospels' description of the agony in the Garden of Gethsemane and which may also reflect Psalm 42, Jesus says: 'Now my soul is in turmoil and what am I to say? Father, save me from this hour. No, it was for this that I came to this hour. Father, glorify thy name' (John 12.27–28). He speaks of death as the glorification. As R. H. Lightfoot writes: 'St John teaches that the Lord's glory is to be fully and finally revealed in the complex of the events of the passion.'[21]

John also uses the deliberately ambiguous term 'lifted up' to describe the crucifixion (John 12.33). It suggests the manner of death, but it also suggests being lifted up or exalted to glory. In the Septuagint the two Greek verbs for 'to be exalted' and 'to be glorified' are used side by side in Isaiah 52.13, of the servant of the Lord.[22]

In his account of Jesus' passion, John emphasizes Jesus' authority. His dying words 'it is accomplished' (19.30) are a cry of victory. John, in C. K. Barrett's phrase, thinks of 'one compound event of crucifixion and resurrection'.[23] The same may be true of Mark's Gospel. If 16.8 is indeed the end of the Gospel, Mark does not include resurrection appearances. The Gospel ends with the women astonished at the empty tomb. Mark's positioning of the Transfiguration as a prologue to his account of the passion points to the same insight as in John's Gospel. A voice from heaven confirms that the one who is about to die is God's Beloved (Mark 9.7). The moment of death is the moment of glory. The power that is revealed on the cross is the power of suffering love.

In Luke's Gospel, by contrast, the moment of revelation is turned into a sequence of 'events' – death, resurrection, ascension. This sequence has been fixed in the consciousness of Christians by liturgical observance and has, in my view, obscured the Johannine teaching. It is likely to suggest that Jesus' exaltation is a reversal of his death and that Jesus' authority replicates that of earthly monarchs. Many hymns are full of triumphalism. They speak of Christ sitting at God's right hand 'till all his foes submit', of kings bowing down to him and of 'kingdom authority flowing to his own' (who have often misused it!).[24]

The resurrection

Often the preaching of the resurrection has mirrored this triumphalism. Alice and Roy Eckardt, two American theologians who have challenged Christians to ponder the Shoah, even say that any continued advocacy of the resurrection appears to represent in clear and authoritative form the fateful, culpable union of the Christian message and the murder camps.[25] They give as an example the writings of the German theologian Wolfhart Pannenberg. Pannenberg held that Jesus clashed with Jewish legalism and that he rejected the Jewish claim that the law contained the eternal will of God in its final formulation. Jesus' claim to the authority of God was, in Pannenberg's view, blasphemous for Jewish ears. Through the resurrection of Jesus, the God of Israel confirmed Jesus' (supposed) view of the law and his claim to divine authority. Pannenberg, therefore, uses the resurrection as evidence that Jesus was right and that Judaism was wrong.[26]

An even more serious misuse of the resurrection, as Paul van Buren makes clear, is to see it as the redemption of the world.

> What it had not accomplished, including such minor details as the end of human suffering, sickness, injustice, oppression and torture, death, much of it horrible . . . all such details were simply scaled down in value in the mythological scenario as being of only transient concern. After all, with eternal life won, why care about actual human life? The more triumphalistic the mythological interpretation of Easter, the more Christianity could calmly ignore the world which it claimed God so loved.[27]

There is in much preaching of the resurrection both a spiritualization and a triumphalism.

St John's integrated understanding of the cross and resurrection suggests that Eastertide sees the dawning conviction that the suffering love shown on the cross is a power stronger than evil and death – that suffering love is the power of God. St Luke tells that on the way to Emmaus, the Risen Jesus explains the necessity of the Messiah's suffering (Luke 24.44–47). In St John's Gospel, the Risen Jesus still bears the marks of the cross (John 20.24–29). Our pain is God's pain. 'The divine glory,' writes Jürgen Moltmann, a leading German theologian, 'is revealed on the face of the crucified Jesus; it no longer belongs to the crowns of kings or the fame of a nation or any other earthly authorities.'[28]

The question at issue is not what happened on Easter Day, but the way in which the resurrection is interpreted. To affirm that Jesus is risen is to affirm also that his way of self-giving love is stronger than evil and is of the nature of reality. Belief in the resurrection implies commitment to the way of life that Jesus expressed and embodied.

The power of suffering love

Images of God's majesty jar, if we are sensitive to the suffering of our world and especially to the horrors of the Shoah. Talking about this at an evening class, one elderly lady who had been a churchgoer all her life, said that for many years she had stopped addressing God as 'Almighty'. Maybe here, too, theology has not caught up with the feelings of some believers.

Yet, if God's power is the power of suffering love, what does this imply? It means that we should abandon pictures of a God with a reserve of power to interfere in the world should he wish to. If God could have intervened, why did God not do so? The inadequacy of old answers can no longer be concealed.[29]

Yet is the power of suffering love a power at all? Why not just abandon belief in God? I doubt whether argument can explicate the basic certainty of faith, which I would describe for myself as being grasped by the love of God in Jesus Christ, symbolized by the cross and the experience, already mentioned, of a peace in the midst of pain.

My understanding of the power of suffering love derives, in part, from an attempt to understand the nature of love as seen at its best in some human lives and then to assume that God's love cannot be less than human love at its highest. In part, as I have already suggested, it is based on a reading of some of the Christian tradition.

The character of authentic love

W. H. Vanstone, an Anglican theologian, in *Love's Endeavour, Love's Expense* suggests three ways in which love is shown to be inauthentic. Love's falsity is unveiled when any limit is set by the will of the one who professes to love, when there is any attempt to control the loved one and if the lover is detached. Authentic love is 'limitless, precarious and vulnerable'.[30] If God's love is limitless, then his love is fully expended in creation. He has no reserve of power with which to intervene and overrule. His love is precarious and therefore the future is not predetermined. Otherwise 'nothing decisive happens and nothing new, it is merely the unwinding and display of a film already made'.[31] Further, God is vulnerable and affected by his creatures.

Such a picture is at variance with traditional definitions of God. Omnipotence has usually implied that God has a reserve of power, even if he chooses to limit his power. Traditional pictures of judgment and hell have suggested a limit to God's love and forgiveness. His omniscience has supposed his foreknowledge of the outcome of human history, thereby depriving humans of creative responsibility for the future. God's impassibility has suggested that he is detached from human pain.

Moltmann writes:

> We must drop the philosophical axioms about the nature of God. God is *not unchangeable*, if to be unchangeable means that he could not in the freedom of his love open himself to the changeable history of his creation. God is *not incapable of suffering*, if this means that in the freedom of his love he would not be receptive to suffering over the contradiction of man and the self-destruction of his creation. God is *not invulnerable*, if this means that he could not open himself to the pain of the cross. God is *not perfect* if this means that he did not in the craving of his love want his creation to be necessary to his perfection.[32]

If God, in his creativity and self-giving, has allowed genuine freedom to the natural world, then it operates according to the 'laws' discerned by scientists. I do not, therefore, think of sudden disasters as 'acts of God', nor could I agree when my children were told at their infant school to pray for a fine day for the church fête. I sympathize with William Temple, then Archbishop of York, when, early in the Second World War, he was horrified to discover that the Archbishop of Canterbury, Cosmo Lang, had said, in the name of both archbishops, 'Do not hesitate to pray for victory.'[33]

God also, I believe, gives freedom to human beings and does not override the consequences of human evil. God's ultimate responsibility for creating a world in which hideous evil is possible cannot be evaded. The extent of evil is the concomitant of freedom.

God seeks to change the world by suffering love. If we had eyes to see, we would see the consequences of our human evil. There is a Bulgarian saying that, 'The living close the eyes of the dead, but the dead open the eyes of the living.'[34]

The victims of war, the children starved to death by hunger, the mutilated corpses of prisoners tortured to death, it is they who should open our eyes to our 'stock-piling guilt',[35] to the selfishness that has propped up Western standards of living by the sale of arms and the silent acquiescence in the hunger of millions. God speaks through the victims to the conscience of the nations.[36] The cruel suffering of so many should lead us to ask again and again: Need it be so? The suffering questions, the complacency and hypocrisy of governments – the lies and ruthlessness by which they remain in power. In this sense, John's Gospel speaks of Jesus' death as the judgment of the world. Human evil and self-deception is shown up in all its ugliness by the cross (John 3.17–21).

Why does God not intervene? To do so would be to coerce. Our good behaviour would be imposed upon us, not freely chosen. The cost is enormous, but we can begin to see that if love is the only power, then that is incompatible with compulsion. Too often we have wanted freedom, but spoken as if God were there to get us out of the mess that we have created.

Our hope, however, is that if God's love is as we picture it here, God will never cease loving until all have been redeemed and creation conformed to his purposes. Love is inherently invincible.

Prayer

Often the way we think about prayer seems to imply that God can save us from the consequences of our actions. Yet prayer should not be an attempt to change God, whose love is unfailing and unceasing, but the willingness to attune ourselves to that love. As we centre ourselves on God, there may indeed be healing (physical as well as spiritual), there will be greater inner peace, there will be strength to struggle on: but the change is in us, as our lives are drawn into harmony with the divine life.

John Austen Baker, Bishop of Salisbury, writes of prayer for others:

> We are not engaged in creating or producing anything, but in becoming aware of what is already the fact, namely that God is immediately and intimately present both to ourselves and to the ones for whom we are praying. Our task is to hold the awareness of this fact in the still centre of our being, to unite our love for them with God's love . . . In technical terms, therefore, intercession is a form of that kind of prayer known as 'contemplation'.[37]

Prayer should not have an expectation that God's will may be altered. That again assumes an 'interventionist' God. Rather, prayer is an attempt to align ourselves with the God whose love is boundless and unceasing.

Our responsibility

The cost of freedom is enormous. One should not suggest that the agony of the victims is 'justified' by any subsequent change in human behaviour. Rather, one must recognize that their agony is the consequence of human evil, often over many years. Tragically it is others who so often pay the cost. The children thrown into the gas ovens were victims of centuries of antisemitism and of anti-Jewish teaching by the churches as well as victims of the cruelty of the Nazis. Centuries of anti-Judaism provided 'the soil in which the evil weed of Nazism was able to take root and spread its poison'.[38] The sins of one generation are visited on their children's children. That bitter history still has its effects in the cruel complexities of the Israeli/Palestinian conflict, as well as in the pain of survivors of the camps.

Our behaviour has deep affects on others. We recognize this in family life and see how deprivation in one generation has its effect on subsequent generations. We do not always see how the society in which we participate has its effect on others. As the world becomes one society we are more aware of this. Our standard of living often rests on the exploitation of others. Imitating a triumphalist God, Western Christians have often looked down on people of other races, colours and religions – even on the fairer sex. The appalling genocide of aboriginal people is one example, mirrored by cruel treatment of animals and by the exploitation of nature.

To picture God as suffering love is to recognize our human selfishness.

The way of non-violence

If God is pictured as suffering love, then faith should commit us to trying to imitate such love. For the Christian, the cross is a call to follow the way of the crucified one, which is the way of non-violent self-giving love. Jesus, as Gandhi said, 'was non-violence *par excellence*'.[39] Pacifism, in the sense of being as non-violent as possible, seems to me integral to the gospel.[40] Discipleship is following one who embodies self-giving non-violent love.

The cross is central to my picture of God, but there are other moments of divine revelation and disclosure. In every faith, and amongst those of no particular religious belief, there are those who sense that love, which gives respect to the other, be they a person of another culture, a victim of human cruelty, or part of the animal creation, characterizes the best of human behaviour and reflects the character of the Transcendent. Participants in the Fifth Assembly of the World Conference on Religion and Peace affirmed at the Melbourne Assembly that 'non-violence is love and love is the most powerful force against injustice and violence'.[41]

Sadly, the record of religions does not confirm this, and human history belies it. Dare we look into the darkness of the Shoah and still affirm the power of self-giving love? There is no external proof of this leap of faith. It is foolishness to the world. Yet to sense a little of the power of such love is to hold on to a hope that God's peace is stronger than the wrath of man and that God's love will not fail until all things are reconciled and made whole. Yet that hope will be realized only as men and women atune themselves to divine love. 'It is man, not God,' says Arthur A. Cohen, an American Jewish thinker, who renders the filament of the divine incandescent or burns it out.'[42] 'We literally hold in our faltering hands,' says Hans Jonas, 'the future of the divine adventure and must not fail Him, even if we would fail ourselves.'[43]

Our own suffering and sensitivity to the agonies of others may make us more aware of our human solidarity and our share of responsibility for shaping humanity's common future. In the creative attempt to do this and to wrest meaning from the heartbreak of so many lives, we may find ourselves at one with a power which is more than human.

Questions

I am left with many questions. It might seem simpler to abandon belief in God than believe in what some would feel was an emasculated Deity. Yet although I have concentrated on suffering, there is also beauty and great joy in life as well as the yearning for 'truth'. There is the mystical sense of peace in and beyond our pain. My hope for the future, too, rests on the conviction that in following the way of suffering love we are in harmony with a power greater than ourselves and that the future is not bounded by this life.

I am conscious that Christian belief, because of the cross, is shaped by a hope that suffering need not be total loss and may be redemptive. I realize that for those who feel that the deaths in the camps were total destruction this may sound heartless, as if the horror has not been fully recognized, and it may seem as if one more Christian is imposing a Christian theological meaning on the sufferings of others. Yet, whilst the Shoah was a Jewish tragedy, it was also a human tragedy. Although dialogue may make us more aware of our particular faith, it also presumes a shared humanity.

It seems that some Jewish thinkers, such as Hans Jonas and Arthur A. Cohen, find themselves picturing God in a similar way. It is a picture that may allow us together, in the shadow of the Shoah, to affirm the power of suffering love and of God's presence in our pain and encourage us to recognize our human responsibility and, fully aware of the cost, together to seek the realization of our messianic hopes.

8. Suffering: A Point of Meeting?

COLIN EIMER

Reading Marcus Braybrooke's chapter, the Jew is aware of the centrality of suffering in Christian thought. How can it be otherwise when the dominant icon that faces the Christian entering church is that of the suffering of Jesus on the cross? How deeply must that image be implanted in the psyche of the Christian? The very title of Marcus's chapter, 'The Power of Suffering Love', employs a vocabulary which does not come readily to Jewish lips.

Jewish views of suffering

The Hebrew Bible has its episodes of suffering, of course. At an individual level, the *dénouement* of the binding of Isaac[1] episode teaches that, ultimately, God does not want that sort of sacrifice. Significantly, in Jewish teaching it is not called 'the sacrifice of Isaac'; that seems more a Christian than a Jewish appellation. But it is also true that in the Middle Ages, when Jewish parents chose to kill their children and themselves rather than die at the hands of the Christian mob, poetic reworkings of that episode turned the 'binding' into 'sacrifice' and 'self-sacrifice'.[2] However, it was seldom taken as an exemplar paradigm of the relationship between God and the Jewish people.

Suffering is scarcely mentioned in the synagogue liturgy. At no point in the Jewish year, for example, does the Book of Job figure in the established lexicon of scriptural readings. In traditional thought, suffering was God's response to Jewish abandonment of the covenant made between the people and God at Mount Sinai. In particular that was the stance adopted by the biblical prophets in attempting to reconcile destruction and exile with God's promise not to abandon the people. Liturgically this is expressed (but only in the High Holyday liturgy) as, 'Because of our sins we were exiled from our land.'[3]

Not even the formative experience of the Jewish people, the slavery in

94

Egypt, is 'used' in the context of a theology of suffering. The key event is the Exodus itself, rather than the slavery that led up to it. This seems a slight, but qualitatively significant, difference of emphasis. The slavery serves as a reminder and imperative to moral behaviour.[4]

The destruction of the Second Temple in the year 70 CE and the accompanying exile led Jews to become self-questioning. Was it our fault that we were exiled, that we suffered this apparent withdrawal of God's love? Many did indeed see it in terms of moral backsliding. Innumerable *midrashim*, biblically based rabbinic homilies, after the year 70 CE, see it in that light.[5]

Does the Shoah raise new questions?

This has therefore been part of normative Jewish theology for centuries. The First World War apart, the Shoah is almost the first event that led Christians to call aspects of their own theology into question. But it is not yet, by any means, a general Christian theological response.

Some years ago Richard Harries, my co-respondent in this section, then Dean of King's College, London, invited me to debate with a young German theologian on the theme of 'Jewish and Christian responses to the Shoah'. The German spoke first and in his lecture referred to many Jewish theologians and their approach to the questions raised by the Shoah. What was most interesting was the response from the audience. Most of the comments were directed to me. Some said, implicitly and explicitly, that the Shoah was brought about by the Jews – and a variety of antisemitic stereotypes were paraded as 'evidence' for that. Others resolutely rejected the suggestion that the Shoah had any implications whatsoever for Christian theology – even though that had been the thrust not only of my remarks but also, more significantly, of those of my Christian debating partner.

To read, therefore, of how the Shoah has lead Marcus to re-examine his own theological stance on God and suffering is welcome. This is of course a parallel to what Jews have been experiencing for forty years or more. Many Jews 'in the street' feel that the Shoah has highlighted the gap between religious teaching and reality, and point to the Shoah as the cause of their loss of faith in God. They ask the questions that Marcus Braybrooke and many Christians ask: how can I continue to affirm God in the way God is traditionally described? What sense does it make to speak of a loving and caring God after the Shoah? How can we talk of an omnipotent God when God was apparently powerless to intervene at Auschwitz?

The Shoah has also led Marcus to re-examine the way in which he enters into dialogue with Jews and Judaism. This too resonates within Jewish experience. But whilst for Marcus and the Christian world it has opened windows on to Jewish-Christian dialogue, for many Jews the comparative silence of the church during the Shoah has closed windows. It 'proves' that there is no point or purpose to the dialogue – can Christians be trusted? The pain and hurt are still too great for any meaningful dialogue to be possible – and my experience at King's College could be quoted as a mundane and prosaic example. What possible point can there be to any dialogue if I am to be told that the Shoah, which included the murder of one million children, is in some way the 'fault' of pre-war European Jewry?

Part of the Jewish world continues to see the Shoah in the light of traditional biblical teaching – it happened because Jews had abandoned the covenant. Jewish attempts to assimilate into Christian Europe brought upon themselves the punishment of God.[6] Some said that Zionism was the cause of the Shoah – it was an idolatry and therefore deserved divine retribution.[7] Others argued precisely the contrary – opposition to Zionism brought about the Shoah because, presumably, many more Jewish lives could have been saved had a Jewish homeland existed.[8] These responses see no need to interpret the Shoah as *sui generis*, unique in any way, and therefore requiring some radical redefinition of existing theological frameworks.

This may seem surprising, given that it was traditional Judaism which suffered most at the hands of the Nazis – the Shoah was most destructive of Jewish life in Eastern Europe, the heartland of Orthodox Judaism. In the discussion that took place in the Jewish world about whether to institute a special Memorial Day to commemorate the Shoah, many traditional thinkers referred to the Talmudic dictum that you do not add new forms of commemoration for more recent disasters.[9] Time needs to elapse before you can evaluate historical experience and translate it into religious certainty. Moreover, days commemorating disasters in Jewish history already exist. In other words, the pattern of non-Jewish persecution of the Jews was established long ago and the Shoah is 'simply' another episode in the continuing saga of antisemitism. Yosef Hayyim Yerushalmi, Professor of Jewish Studies at Columbia University, New York, provides an example of this in his book *Zakhor*.[10] Hillel Goldberg, an American Orthodox rabbi, sums up this whole approach when he writes: 'To be unique, the Shoah would have to be beyond interpretation, beyond response, beyond attempts to integrate it into the long chain of Jewish faith. It is precisely the survivors' attempts at interpretation, response, integration that robs the Holocaust of its uniqueness.'[11] Norman Solomon has similarly argued that whilst the Shoah might have been historically unique, it is not unique theologically. The questions it poses 'were there all the time. The Shoah has focused our attention on them as never before, but they are the same questions.'[12] He suggests that modern thinkers have distanced themselves from existing theologies of suffering for two reasons. Traditional responses were seldom satisfactory and were called into question even at the time they were being formulated. Theology had been in a state of ferment anyway for nigh on a century before the Shoah. All it did was administer the *coup de grâce* to traditional attitudes. Previous traumatic episodes of disaster and persecution[13] did not need new theologies, but could be subsumed under traditional patterns of response.

Norman Solomon's distinction between historical and theological uniqueness seems, however, somewhat artificial. For if theology is the attempt to reconcile teaching with reality, and theological development takes place when there are radical changes in reality, then the historical uniqueness of the Shoah must call into question previously-adopted theological stances. Norman Solomon uses a 'hard cases don't make good law' argument to caution against using the Shoah as the basis on which to re-examine traditional beliefs. 'Serious intellectual issues of faith in the modern world,' he argues, 'thereby become submerged in a deep emotional trauma which prevents their being directly faced.'[14] Whilst we can recognize the concern behind the *caveat*, it surely cannot be used to still theological questioning.

Jewish responses to the Shoah

Among non-traditional theologians, Ignaz Maybaum, a German-born British Reform rabbi, is virtually alone in arguing that the Shoah can fit into existing frameworks. He called it the Third *Churban*, the word used by Rabbinic Judaism to describe the destruction of the Temples.[15] He argues that each of these traumatic moments in Jewish history has been a turning point in some way, an opportunity, ultimately, for growth, development and progress. He is less specific about how the Shoah fits into that schema, but does speak of it as 'the end of the Middle Ages', suggesting that the European diaspora has become a world diaspora, and that greater freedom for people has emerged. Maybaum has generally been ignored or attacked, most notably by the American Professor Steven Katz, who argues that it is a theological outrage to suggest that the Shoah resulted in progress and greater freedom. Better none of that than the Shoah.[16]

The American Orthodox rabbi Irving Greenberg might not use the word 'progress' when talking of the Shoah, but he suggests that it has led to a redefinition of the covenant with God. The Shoah could understandably have led to a massive defection from any involvement with covenantal obligations. 'But the overwhelming majority of survivors, far from yielding to despair, rebuilt Jewish lives and took part in the assumption of power by the Jewish people . . . By every right, the Jews should have questioned or rejected the covenant . . . In fact, the bulk of Jews, observant and non-observant alike, acted to recreate the greatest Biblical symbol validating the covenant, the State of Israel.'[17] For Greenberg, then, the assumption of power by the Jews, as embodied in the state of Israel, is the progress that has emerged out of the destruction of the Shoah.

A number of thinkers represent the major Jewish responses to the Shoah. Elie Wiesel and other survivors speak eloquently of the need to bear witness. It is through memory that there lies the possibility of ensuring that such an event never happens again – not just to Jews but to anybody. But there can be no 'explanation' for the Shoah.

What of God's 'involvement' in it? Wiesel relates how at a public hanging at Auschwitz he came to see that God was also, as it were, hanging there. But it is unclear if he means that God is dead, or that it is better to be amongst the persecuted than the persecutors, or that a limited God is better than an impotent God. He also describes how, in one camp he was in, God was put on trial for what was happening to the Jews – and was found guilty. But then the participants remembered it was time for evening prayers and everybody went to pray. The patterns of Jewish life must continue – however difficult that may be, the idea of any alternative is worse still.[18]

Richard Rubenstein would argue that it is impossible to speak of a benevolent omnipotent God after the Shoah. 'The thread uniting God and man, heaven and earth, has been broken. We stand in a cold, silent, unfeeling cosmos, unaided by any purposeful power beyond our own resources. After Auschwitz, what else can a Jew say about God?'[19] Jewish teaching was unable to provide mechanisms of responding to it because it had produced an attitude of quiescent acceptance. All that is left is simple human connectedness. 'I do not believe that a theistic God is necessary for Jewish religious life. Bonhoeffer has written that our problem is how to speak of God in an age of no religion. I believe that our problem is how to speak of religion in an age of no God.'[20]

Emil Fackenheim has long argued that the uniqueness of the Shoah means that traditional responses are inadequate – we cannot go on living simply as before. Yet Auschwitz would seem to suggest that Jewish life has no meaning. For Fackenheim, the resolution of this contradiction is to make continued survival and existence into a theological imperative.[21] He suggests that the gap between believer and agnostic after Auschwitz is quite close – for different reasons, both find it hard to experience God after Auschwitz. In subsequent writing he develops the rabbinic idea of *tikkun olam*, 'setting the world to rights', as a response to the Nazi logic of destruction. 'We are under orders to live,' he writes, accepting that there is a rupture between pre- and post-Shoah theology. The 'Holocaust universe must be resisted in flesh and blood action and life'.[22]

Is there a sense, then, in which a Jew can talk of the power of suffering love? If we speak of a God who cares, who loves his people, of God as a loving parent, then we have also to speak of God who suffers. In the same breath that the biblical prophets establish a connection between abandonment of the covenant and consequent suffering, they also speak of God's continuing love. The *Shekhinah*, the divine presence, has gone into exile with the people. God will be with them, will not abandon them and will ultimately return them to their land and former glory. To match the tears we weep by the waters of Babylon, God also weeps.

It is in the 2000-year-old tradition of midrash, the world of homily and parable, of the 'God, as it were' analogy, that we find this idea most fully developed. Rabbi Jose, relates one midrash, entered the ruins of the Temple in Jerusalem. He wept there for the glory that was lost. In the midst of his anguish, he heard a *bat kol*, a voice from heaven, lamenting: 'Woe is me, for I have destroyed my house, burned my Temple, and exiled my children!'[23]

Out of such statements developed the idea of *hester panim*, the idea that God, as it were, hides his face. This can be understood in a number of ways. God hides his face, turns away from the people because of the wrong they do. God can no longer tolerate what his people have done and turns away, angry and disappointed. That was the sense of abandonment the people felt at the time of the exile.

Such a view posits a God like the parents of a very young child. When they see the child moving towards danger they rush over and rescue it. But children must grow up and bear the consequences of their actions. They move beyond direct parental intervention. The parents can only watch in pain and anguish as their loved child damages itself in some way. But they can do no more. That, too, is part of *hester panim*. God is not angry or disappointed, but constrained by human freedom – the very power he has granted to his creation. It is not free-will at all if we expect God to bail us out when things go wrong. If there is *hester panim*, turning away, it is to hide the grief and pain at what humans do. Even the enormity of the Shoah is beyond his reach. Like the earthly parent, all he can do is suffer in silence and be there – accessible to his beloved children should they wish to come to him.

That theme is powerfully picked up in the Jewish mystical tradition with the concept of *tzimtzum*, 'limitation and withdrawal'. In creating the world, God could only make space for human beings by a voluntary withdrawal. As was recently stated: 'Thus was created that space which is

99

necessary for the endless number of possibilities that make up life. In that space, it would seem, chance events occur and human creativity (I would want to add 'and human destructiveness') is allowed for. There is no place where God is not, but God's presence is not to be identified with the miraculous abrogation of the laws of physics or of the natural world.[24]

Irving Greenberg, already referred to, puts this sense of God's withdrawal into a slightly different theological frame. Human history, he argues, is the record of God's progressive withdrawal, the transfer of power and authority from divine to human hands, so that we take more and more responsibility for our situation and circumstances.[25] Until the Shoah, there was little that was voluntary in it. The Shoah changed all that. 'In the covenant, the Jews were called as witness to the world for God and for a final perfection. In the light of the Holocaust, it is obvious that this role opened the Jews to a murderous fury from which there was no escape. Yet the divine could not or would not save them from this fate . . . Morally speaking, then, God can have no claims on the Jews by dint of the covenant. The fundamental shift in the nature of the covenant can be put yet another way. It can no longer be commanded . . . If the Jews keep the covenant after the Holocaust, then it can no longer be for the reason that it is commanded or because it is enforced by reward or punishment.'[26] For Greenberg, then, the greatest 'surprise' to emerge from the Shoah is not that some Jews have abandoned their now voluntary covenantal obligations, but rather that so many continue to affirm those responsibilities – working for the rebuilding of Israel; a massive Jewish involvement in all ways, in all societies, working for that *tikkun olam* about which Fackenheim writes.

Arthur Cohen, in a closely-argued essay,[27] refers to the Shoah as the *tremendum*. He borrows the phrase from Rudolf Otto's *mysterium tremendum* because it encompasses a sense both of vastness and of terror. Cohen wants to draw only the most cautious and tentative conclusions from the Shoah. 'We are on the bridge over the abyss, not in the abyss itself.'[28] But we have looked into the abyss. This means we can no longer glibly account God as good, as classical theism asserts; nor, on the other hand, can we argue that God is dead, for that would be no more than 'trifling narcissism'.[29] To argue that God was silent during the Shoah rests, says Cohen, on too many shaky assumptions: that God only spoke to previous generations and in human language; that God's speaking automatically means God's acting, which in turn automatically means God's redeeming. 'If we can see God less as the interferer, more as the immensity whose reality is our prefiguration, whose speech and silence are metaphors for our language and distortion, whose plenitude and unfolding are the hope of our futurity, we shall have won a sense of God whom we may love and honour, but whom we no longer fear and from whom we no longer demand.'[30] Cohen introduces a striking image in his attempt to understand a God who creates a universe in which the destructiveness of the Shoah can happen. It is that of the filament of a light bulb. 'It is linked to the historical, but separate from it, for history is the domain of human freedom.'[31] But it is human beings who can render the filament of the divine incandescent or who can eclipse, obscure or burn it out. In the Shoah, it risked being burned out. Cohen offers a way, therefore, in which we can cease to see God as interventionist, can move beyond that imagery and struggle to 'find the terms to renew the meaning of creation and authenticate the promise of redemption'.[32]

Can we join hands?

There are many ways, therefore, whereby a Jewish and a Christian response to the Shoah can join hands. But where we would part company is when, for example, Marcus Braybrooke writes of 'the glory of the cross'. In Jewish thinking the words 'pain' and 'suffering' sit very uncomfortably with the word 'glory' – divine or human. The cross and the resurrection have been, and still are, used to preach Christian triumphalism, 'proofs' of the rightness of the Christian message. One of the dangers of such triumphalism, of course, is the coercive imperative many feel it bestows. The connection between universalism and despotism is well-established – if you feel you have the truth for all humanity, you will not be over-concerned if, along the way, you have to coerce a few people to accept your truth.

Marcus suggests that 'non-violent, self-giving love' is a human expression of *imitatio Dei*, citing Gandhian *satyagraha* as the model. But the Shoah gave the lie to non-violence. It works on the assumption that adversaries have moral limits, lines that even they will not cross, and confronts them with those limits. The Nazis, however, knew no such boundaries and were unfettered by any moral considerations. When that situation exists, non-violent resistance becomes almost suicidal, and loses touch with reality. A fortnight after *Kristallnacht* Gandhi could still write in his newspaper column: 'If someone with courage and vision can arise among the Jews of Germany to lead them in non-violent action, the winter of their despair can in the twinkling of an eye be turned into the summer of hope. What has today become a degrading man-hunt can be turned into a calm and determined stand offered by unarmed men and women possessing the strength of suffering given to them by Jehovah.'[33] What would he have advocated at the height of the actual extermination programme?

Inter-faith dialogue is a curious business. It is so hard to play it by the 'rules'[34] and grow beyond scoring points or trying to fit what the other says into one's own religious framework. There is a common, shared vocabulary – of covenant, witness, serving the Lord, chosenness, truth, Messiah and so on. So often we can walk along the same path together in integrity. But then suddenly one trips up over a nuance of different meaning and interpretation. We recognize our commonality – but also our difference. Can Marcus ever fully understand what 'Torah' means to me? Can I ever understand what 'the cross' represents for Marcus? Inevitably, there will always be that aspect of 'blindness' to the totality of what our respective traditions mean for each of us. For some that is a perpetual barrier; for us it has become a bridge, enabling us to clarify our perception of the other and hone up our self-understanding.

In the face of suffering, we can both speak of hope – for Marcus of a Second Coming, for me of The Coming. The devout Jew repeats Maimonides' formulation daily: 'I believe with perfect faith in the coming of the messiah – and though he tarry, I still believe.' It is reported that Jews sang those words in the gas-chambers of Auschwitz – not blind faith, surely, for there can be none of that at such a moment, but a certainty of sorts. The Jew lives daily on the edge of that hope, and (or but) does not despair at midnight when it has not happened.

There are no escape routes: into despair or negation; into trite answers or blind acceptance; or into any glorification of suffering. 'Few are the men,' concludes Primo Levi, an Italian survivor of the Shoah, in his reflections on Auschwitz, 'who draw moral strength from failure.'[35] There is, moreover, a gap between liturgical models and those we live with in everyday reality. We can speak of a 'God of history', but only at the risk of becoming manic-depressive: 'He loves me, he loves me not'. Leo Baeck recognized the need for different theological models after the Shoah. Before the war, he referred to God as 'Der Ewige', 'the Eternal One' – the transcendent, remote God, the God of the philosophers; after the war, after his experience in Terezin, he reportedly only referred to God as 'Er, der ist', 'He who is' – immanent, close, the God of personal experience.[36] In some sense, I feel almost 'jealous' that Christianity has what appears to be a ready-made theological framework into which suffering can be subsumed. Yet that also seems just a bit too easy, because it can degenerate into no more than a religious 'comfort-blanket' to smother self-questioning. Given Judaism's historical experience of persecution it is surprising, perhaps, that it has not concentrated more on working out a systematic theology of suffering. David Hartman, an American-born Israeli theologian, suggests that this is 'not because the rabbis could not think in a coherent philosophical way, but because systematic theology could not do justice to the vitality and complexity of experience'.[37] What it can and did do was to develop a theology of living, expressed, both during and since the Shoah, in terms of *kiddush ha'hayyim*, the 'sanctification of life'.[38]

Here, too, in the face of human suffering, we have to recognize our limitations. This is part of not accepting trite responses, for in the face of the mystery, any response can only be partial and lead to more questions. 'Religion offers answers without obliterating the questions. They become blunted and will not attack you with the same ferocity. But without them the answer would dry up and wither away. The question is a great religious act; it helps you live great religious truth.'[39]

Suffering is part of the 'birthright' of all people. Judaism can speak of a God who suffers *with* his creation but not *for*, or *on behalf of* it. God is the great Unity and the great Unifier. In our dialogue we can come together to hear the authentic voice of the Other. Together we can grope, in humility, towards a deeper shared understanding. Together we can evolve a vocabulary which is rigorous enough to stand up to the questions raised by the Shoah and the experience of suffering. The most minimalist lesson to be drawn from the Shoah must be that 'tired', trite pre-Shoah theology and theological categories are simply inadequate to face up to what the Shoah represents. A generation ago, we saw the 'filament of the divine' almost extinguished by human action. Nazi propaganda and Nazi decrees sought to create a social distance between the Jew and the rest of humanity. When that distance exists, what is normally unacceptable becomes acceptable. Our dialogue has been part of the attempt to overcome the polarizing forces which would still wish to create that social gap. Out of that we can come to work together to relieve those areas of suffering where we have the possibility of action – to fight evil, to help those who suffer, to realize in concrete action our nature as 'co-partners with God' in the work of *tikkun olam*, of setting the world to rights.

9. Theodicy will not Go Away

RICHARD HARRIES

In his sensitive and deeply-felt chapter Marcus Braybrooke locates his sense of God in the experience of shared suffering. When ministering to people in anguish, he has been conscious of a divine presence who enters into our suffering and helps us to bear the burdens of others. As a Christian he finds this presence focussed in the figure of Christ crucified. It is this awareness which enables him to avoid atheism whilst at the same time rejecting some traditional understandings of faith.

One element of traditional theology he rejects is theodicy, that is, intellectual attempts to reconcile belief in a God of love with the presence of so much anguish in the world. Indeed, he follows Dorothee Sölle in regarding the familiar questions of theodicy as fundamentally misconceived.

The questions will not go away

The questions will not, however, go away so easily. For the God who meets us as we enter into the affliction of the world is also the God who moment by moment holds this very world in being. Without this power of being, which lets us be, there would be no me or you or anyone. Here, very often we find ourselves conscious of life as a blessing for which we want to give heartfelt thanks and sometimes overwhelmed by the sheer cruelty and misery of the world, wondering how there could possibly be a good God behind it at all. Such questions are not the invention of theologians. They arise in the mind of all who wish to sustain faith in the midst of human misery. There has, in fact, been some outstanding Christian writing on the questions of theodicy in recent decades.[1] The considerations there adduced are not usually appropriate in a pastoral setting, nor are they a substitute for the practical responses that are required of us, nor do they give complete answers. But they enable us to go on in faith and hope, as well as love. As such, a sound theodicy, far from being misconceived or an optional extra to faith, is an essential aspect of any belief that seeks to commend itself to reasonable minds, including our own. The prime requirement is to be pastorally sensitive and responsive to the actual character of human existence in all its complexity, and ambiguity. As Colin Eimer powerfully puts it: 'There are no escape routes: into despair or negation; into trite answers or blind acceptance; or into any glorification of suffering' (p. 102). He quotes David Hartman, who believes that the rabbis did not concentrate more on working out a systematic theology of suffering because such a systematic theology could not do justice to the vitality and complexity of experience, and then the Czech refugee and rabbi Shmuel Sperber: 'Religion offers answers without obliterating the questions. They become blunted and will not attack you with the same ferocity. But without them the answer would dry up and wither away. The question is a great religious act; it helps you live great religious truth.' Here one is reminded not only of Job, who relentlessly pursued his questioning to the very face of God, despite all attempts of those with tidy answers to get him to accept them, but of Elie Wiesel who as a boy used to talk to the Beadle in his synagogue. The Beadle would say to him:

> Man raises himself toward God by the questions he asks him. That is the true dialogue. Man questions God and God answers. But we don't understand his answers. We can't understand them. Because they come from the depth of the soul, and they stay there until death. You will find the true answers, Eliezer, only within yourself!

When Eliezer asks why the Beadle prays he is told: 'I pray to the God within me that he will give me the strength to ask him the right questions.'[2] This emphasis on questioning seems, to a Christian, very Jewish, and an aspect of the faith from which we could learn and by which we could be enriched. It stands in contrast to the Christian tendency to systematize.

All this having been said, however, there remains the question about the ground of our hope. Why should we continue to hope that there is a wise and loving power behind this strange, painful and beautiful universe of ours?

All that Marcus so strongly and rightly says of Christian responsibility for Jewish suffering accentuates the problem of theodicy for Christians in two ways. First, the enormity of the evil we have to contemplate. Jews have to reconcile their own suffering with a God of love. Christians have not only their own suffering to consider but that which they themselves have inflicted. Furthermore, they have to face the fact that the incarnation of God's Son, giving rise to the Christian movement in history, has had the dire result of bringing about so much suffering. In one of his poems, R. S.

Thomas imagines Christ contemplating the world before the Incarnation. He sees human beings suffering: 'Let me go there, he said.'[3] But in the light of what we now know he would have to contemplate not only human suffering but suffering consequent upon his coming amongst us.

Ivan Karamazov did not think God was justified in creating the world, even though an ultimate harmony might be achieved, if children had to suffer in the process.[4] If that final redemption is brought about by a divine incarnation which has as one of its unintended consequences the teaching of contempt by the Christian church, and a Christian Europe which failed to prevent the Shoah, Ivan Karamazov's point applies with new force both to the creation and the incarnation.

Secondly, continuing Jewish faith in God both in and after the Holocaust is a most powerful witness. Despite such horrendous suffering, despite the elimination of virtually all Jewish life in Germany and so much of Eastern Europe, many Jewish people continue to affirm the existence of the Holy One and work in many practical ways for the realization of his kingdom.

The problem of theodicy is posed by the fact that life is such an inextricable mixture of happiness and misery. If life were entirely a burden, the problem of theodicy would not arise. We would know it was the product of an evil or indifferent power. It is because (at least for some of the time) we experience life as a blessing and want to give thanks to a good creator that the evil we see around us appears as such a contradiction of what we otherwise know. The questions that lie behind traditional theodicy, far from being misconceived, take on, in the light of the Shoah, a new intensity for Christians. The evil we have to face is not just an evil permitted by God but one that came into the world in the wake of Christ's Incarnation. The faith we have to go on is not just our own but that of the Jewish people, who despite everything continue to bless God for their creation.

It is clear that in their respective responses to the problem of evil Jews and Christians will want to say many of the same things, even though sometimes in different language. Christians talk about God's will to create beings with genuine free choice and the limitations this imposes on what God can do without contradicting his fundamental purpose. The Jewish mystical tradition suggests that God could only make space for human beings by a voluntary withdrawal. Within the all-embracing cape of his presence he makes a small space where he is not, in order that human beings might be with a life of their own. So as Colin Eimer rightly says, God watches over us in pain and anguish as we his loved children damage ourselves and one another. But God cannot simply bale us out when things go wrong. 'Like the earthly parent, all he can do is suffer in silence and be there – accessible to his beloved children should they wish to come to him'

(p. 99). Yet God does do more than this. He is ceaselessly active, seeking to draw good out of evil and inviting us to co-operate with him in the task. He does not do this in a remote and distanced manner but, through his spirit, from within the flux of human events. For he is with us and for us, striving in our striving, suffering in our suffering.

It is the nature of love to enter into and share the suffering of others. With Marcus's emphasis on this, every Christian will agree. One of the valuable insights that has come to me out of my membership of the Manor House Group is the awareness of how much this understanding of God is also present within the Jewish tradition.[5] The question arises, however, whether it is adequate to talk about 'the power of suffering love' without further analysis of the kind of power that quite properly belongs to God as God.[6]

Power is the capacity to achieve certain goals. We all have a certain power as human beings or else we would simply drop down and die. We can use that power in loving or unloving ways, but we cannot escape the fact that we have power. It is a mistake to think of God as being totally powerless. God has all the power that belongs to God as God. He has the power to create *ex nihilo*. He also has the power to recreate. He has the power to work in and through his creation to bring all things to their appointed end. God pours himself into his creation, as W. H. Vanstone's book so movingly explores,[7] but God's reserves of himself are inexhaustible. He ceaselessly works, at every point in the universe, for the fulfilment of his purpose by drawing good out of evil. In short, God is not, in the philosopher A. N. Whitehead's phrase, simply the fellow sufferer who understands. He is God the creator, who, at terrible risk, brings this world into being but who does so with a reasonable hope of bringing it to a successful outcome, that is, the growth, spiritual development and eternal fulfilment of his creatures. Otherwise, creation would have been a totally irresponsible act. It is a wounded surgeon who plies the steel, as T. S. Eliot so vividly put it.[8] But a surgeon is more than someone who shares our suffering. He takes action for our good.

Colin Eimer writes that after reading Marcus's chapter, 'The Jew is aware of the centrality of suffering in Christian thought. How can it be otherwise when the dominant icon that faces the Christian entering the church is that of the suffering of Jesus on the cross?' (p. 94). But the iconography of the early church was very different. The first scene of Christ on the cross does not appear until the fifth century. Before that time the main images were ones of deliverance. Sometimes the motifs were those of late antiquity, but they are predominantly drawn from the Hebrew scriptures and include such scenes as Daniel in the lion's den; Shadrach, Meshach and Abednego being delivered from the burning fiery furnace;

and the story of Jonah, which ends in triumph and which the early church took as a foreshadowing of the death and resurrection of Christ. From the gospel it was above all the scenes of the raising of Lazarus and the healing of the paralytic that appeared.

Life beyond the grave

When Christ is first depicted on the cross, as in a series of four ivory panels dating from about 420 CE in the British Museum, he is strong and triumphant. Christ as a suffering, battered figure did not emerge for a further 400 years. What spoke to the condition of Christians in the first 900 years was the strong Christ who saves us from fate, evil, all forms of malevolent power and death.

It is quite clear that millions of people do not find their proper fulfilment in this life. They die young, are born mentally ill, are crushed by circumstances and so on. If there is a loving and wise power behind this strange life of ours then his purposes cannot be limited to this earth. There must be the possibility of further growth, especially in the knowledge and love of God himself, beyond the spatio-temporal order. As the Vatican discussion of liberation theology puts it:

> For true justice must include everyone; it must bring the answer to the immense load of suffering born by all the generations. In fact without the resurrection of the dead and the Lord's judgement, there is no justice in the full sense of the term. The promise of the resurrection is freely made to meet the desire for true justice dwelling in the human heart.[9]

Dan Cohn-Sherbok in his clear exposition and critique of Jewish Holocaust theology[10] points out that all its representatives fail to take hope of an after-life seriously and that without this it is difficult to see how faith after the Shoah can be sustained. Despite the fact that many Jews and Christians seem able to believe in God whilst at the same time sitting very light to the possibility of an after-life, Rabbi Cohn-Sherbok is surely correct. The God who creates us also has the power to recreate us. Being a God of love he wills to do just this. Our essential self is known to him. His knowledge of us does not die. He will refashion and reclothe us, though in what form we do not know.

Over the last hundred years such a faith has been rejected by Freud as wishful thinking and by Marx as a misplaced social hope. Such charges need to be taken seriously, but if they are, they can be answered in a way that is reasonable. For Christians, this recreation, this beginning of a new heaven and a new earth has begun in the resurrection of Jesus Christ from the dead. The cross and the resurrection must indeed be seen together, as is the case in John's Gospel, and as Marcus wishes to stress. Nevertheless, the resurrection of Christ is not simply a particular way of looking at the cross. It is more than a change in the hearts of the disciples from seeing the cross as a defeat to affirming it as a victory. It is an event at once within and beyond history. There are difficulties in this position, historical, moral and theological, but I believe they can be met.[11] The particular difficulty in relation to Jewish-Christian dialogue is how can we talk about the resurrection of Christ without being triumphalistic towards our Jewish brothers and sisters. Indeed Alice and Roy Eckhardt believe, wrongly in my view, that it is impossible to do this without implying supersessionism.[12] But the resurrection of Christ is not only the validation of his person but of his faith. His faith was a total trust in the God of Abraham, Isaac and Jacob. The resurrection validates his life as a Jew obedient to the Torah and so validates every Jewish life of obedience and hope.

The hope we share

For hope is one of the vital elements which Jews and Christians share in their response to suffering and the Shoah. As the Chief Rabbi Dr Jonathan Sacks said in conversation, this is neither the best of all possible worlds nor the worst of all possible worlds but 'the worst of all possible worlds – in which there is hope'. As the 1988 Lambeth Conference of Anglican Bishops put it:

> Christians and Jews share one hope, which is for the realization of God's Kingdom on earth. Together they wait for it, pray for it and prepare for it. This Kingdom is nothing less than human life and society transformed, transfigured and transparent to the glory of God. Christians believe that this glory has already shone in the face of Jesus Christ. In his life, death and resurrection the Kingdom of God, God's just rule, has already broken into the affairs of this world. Judaism is not able to accept this. However, Christian belief in Jesus is related to a frame of reference which Christians and Jews share. For it is as a result of incorporation into Jesus Christ that Christians come to share in the Jewish hope for the coming of God's Kingdom.[13]

On Karl Marx's grave in Highgate Cemetery are carved the words 'Philosophers have only interpreted the world; the point is, however, to change it'. With that sentiment both other Jews and Christians would agree. We are not concerned so much with the meaning of life as for the realization of God's purposes in relation to the whole of his creation. We look for the coming of his kingdom, his just and gentle rule. So we seek to stand together in practical endeavour of all kinds, the well-being of the Jewish community, upholding human rights wherever they are violated and working for the elimination of poverty both in this country and amongst the one billion people in the world now living at or below starvation level. There is practical work to be done together. There is also for the Christian community a particular responsibility at this time for correcting in its teachings all distortions of Judaism. I am conscious of how much I myself have needed to be re-educated. I am afraid that for the church as a whole there is still a massive task to be done.

Remembering the Shoah

Clifford Longley has written, in relation to the Shoah, that 'One day even mourning must end.'[14] He suggested that the millions of Jews killed by the Nazis should not be seen simply from a Jewish perspective but should be regarded as a crime against humanity by all decent people. He suggested further that continued Jewish preoccupation with the Shoah tended to distort Jewish-Christian relations and in particular an objective view of the State of Israel. In short, the time of mourning should come to an end. Understandably, there was a fierce reaction from some members of the Jewish community.

It would be impertinent and condescending of any Gentile to suggest to the Jewish community when a time of mourning should end. But from a Christian point of view it needs to be asserted that memory of the Shoah needs to be kept alive and thought of as a crucial event in human history. We need to be continually reminded, until the end of the ages, of the depths of depravity to which human beings can sink unless they take steps to guard against it, and in particular we need to be aware of the terrible consequences of certain tendencies within Christianity unless positive action to counteract them is taken. The Shoah may or may not pose any new questions for theodicy. But it ensures that the old questions, in particular the old question of Christianity's relation to Judaism, and the consequences of this, continue to be faced.

Because of his aim of creating free beings, God does not always succeed in preventing evil. But he is ceaselessly at work bringing good out of evil through the willing co-operation of those striving to do his will. A new relationship with Judaism is one urgent good that the church needs to wrest, through the grace of God, from the sorry story of the past.

Part Four
Religion and the Transformation of Society

10. Jews and Christians: A Shared Social Responsibility

JULIA NEUBERGER

Pulpit and hustings

On so many occasions, and particularly when general elections loom up in the last year or so of a government's term, lectures are given or seminars are held entitled 'Judaism and Politics', or 'The Natural Stance of the Jew in Politics is on the Left', or 'Judaism and Human Rights', and so on. Christian colleagues have the same experience, but it goes further. In election campaigns they often host within their churches a cross-party debate on a variety of issues. When I was standing for Parliament in 1983, there were debates in eight parish churches within and on the edge of the constituency. There was the clergy vote. Some removed their dog-collars and came to campaign on the other side of the constituency where they would not be recognized. Others passed little notes out of their churches, 'We clergy must stick together . . .' It began to look like, 'The natural stance of the clergy in politics is in the middle, particularly if they are supporting another clergyperson . . .'

So what is the mission of our two religions in this world, in the political and moral hurly-burly that is sometimes called debate? More particularly, should clergy and rabbis take part in political debate? Is it true that, as those with a sharpened moral sensitivity suggest, we should have a 'bias to the poor'? If so, what does that mean for the rich? Are we biased against them? In this officially Christian country, where wealth has grown rapidly, particularly for those aged between twenty-five and forty-five, charitable giving has not kept pace with inflation. Those who have made most out of the boom years of the 1980s give least to charity. Is that something on which our religious traditions have much to say?

There were, and are, all the messages about how the clergy – in the broadest sense, including rabbis – should not preach politics from the pulpit. There was the sense of increasing alienation of those whose views were well to the right, or well to the left. In the case of the Church of

England there was an outcry of mammoth proportions when the then Archbishop of Canterbury, Dr Robert Runcie, introduced and publicly supported the conclusions of his commission's working party on the inner city, *Faith in the City*.[1] The national press lambasted the report as communist; it displayed a 'bias to the poor'. This was not the stuff of Christianity, this was Marxism.

Here, of course, was the Church of England using the prophetic tradition to be fearless in criticizing both the political stances and, more profoundly, the underlying social attitudes that made such human misery and degradation possible. But there is an essential difference between what it is possible to find in Christianity about a special relationship between the divine and the poverty-stricken and what one finds in Judaism. At about the same time, Jonathan Sacks, now himself Chief Rabbi, wrote a pamphlet entitled *Wealth and Poverty: A Jewish Response*,[2] for the Social Affairs Unit, an essentially right-wing think tank headed by Dr Digby Anderson. In it he pointed out quite rightly that Judaism regards poverty as an unmitigated evil, and that God is the spokesman for the poor only in the sense of being their champion when they are oppressed. There is no virtue in embracing poverty, in abandoning worldly goods, or in asceticism, which implies a disavowal of this world, the world made by God for us to enjoy. There is no Jewish equivalent of the Franciscan ideal of poverty, and Salo Baron, author of the vast and authoritative *Social and Religious History of the Jews*,[3] makes it clear that,

> There was nothing in that book (the book of the Pious), a thirteenth-century work often cited as a Jewish lay pietistic work with an ascetic streak, which resembled the early Christian and Franciscan ideals of poverty. All that mattered was honesty in dealing with both Jews and Gentiles and charitableness in dispensing the fruits of one's labours.

Sacks, with others, has classed this as a central plank in Jewish thought, and it is unchallengeable. To fight for the poor, to be on their side, to regard poverty as an 'unmitigated evil', does not mean that we have to join them, or to regard God as being towards them, or favouring them over the rich. It has quite different implications for the duty of the rich towards the poor, and an essentially communitarian view of society, rather than an individualistic one such as some strands of Christianity have embraced, suggesting that how each member of a society behaves and relates to other members of that same society has a profound effect on its fabric.

If one combines this with Lord Jakobovits' view that the proper thing to do about poverty is to encourage the poor to stand on their own two feet, to pull themselves up by their bootstraps and get themselves established as independent, without a critique of what brought them into poverty in the first place (despite the duty of the rich to help the poor and show them care and concern), one can see how during the late 1980s the picture presented to the public of the Jewish response to these social issues was deeply congenial to some conservative views of the time, and how it came to be the case that Tory ministers, in the House of Commons, were quoting with approbation what they took to be a classic Jewish view.

Take for instance the former Cabinet Minister Kenneth Baker, quoting from *From Doom to Hope*, the then Chief Rabbi's response to *Faith in the City*:

A Jewish religious contribution would lay greater emphasis on building up self-respect by encouraging ambition and enterprise . . . let them (parents) encourage ambition and enterprise in every negro child as Jewish parents encouraged in their children and they will pull down their ghetto walls as surely as we demolished ours.[4]

The furore about *Faith in the City* was undoubtedly fuelled by Lord Jakobovits, who cited his own very different views on the inner city, views in themselves often very different from those of many other Jews – certainly from mine. His view as to what a Jewish response to these issues might be is utterly different from what we might hear from many Jewish MPs or Jewish lawyers, or many progressive, and indeed Orthodox, rabbis.

Was this, is this, a vision for this world? Or is it one of a series of possible visions for this world where there are any number of political stances, most of which, to some extent or other, can be made to accord with the underlying thrust, moral and political, of religious institutions? Or is the distinction a very different one, between a religious grouping such as Judaism, that regards individuals as essentially part of community, that fundamentally has little concept of individual salvation, and one such as Christianity, where the individual route to salvation is well marked, and although there are community duties, the sense of the individual's role, and the individual's own religious path, is much greater than it is in Judaism.

It is no coincidence that one finds in Jewish thought comments such as: 'It is as if there are men in a boat, and one man takes an auger and begins to bore a hole underneath his seat. His companions say to him: "What are you doing?" He replies: "What business is it of yours? Am I not only boring under my seat?" They answer: "It is our business, because the water will come in and swamp the boat with us in it." '[5] We are all in it together. Of course a sense of mutual obligation is to be found in Christianity as well, but it is hugely emphasized in Judaism, giving Jews a particular stance about social issues, if no others, within society.

It is much more difficult for Church of England colleagues. They are part of an established church. Some of their bishops sit as of right in the House of Lords, and those who are not yet bishops may not stand for Parliament. They are part of the constitutional fabric of British society. They are, in modern parlance, official stakeholders in the political process, and in one way at least excluded from it. Yet they are expected, in some curious, unspecified way, to uphold the moral fabric of society. It is not clear that they are expected to have a vision of society as such, but – at least as it would appear from reading some parts of the popular and quality press – they are expected to have an essentially conservative view, to maintain the picture of England as it was (if it ever was) as a 'green and pleasant land', wherein no trouble lies.

This does not apply to Jews or non-conformists. Lord Jakobovits did not come to sit in the House of Lords by virtue of being Chief Rabbi, but because his vision of Britain, his moral stance, seemed deeply congenial to Mrs Thatcher when she was Prime Minister. In Peregrine Worsthorne's memorable words: 'Judging by the language of the Christian Bishops, Catholic as much as Anglican, this government is bent on doing the Devil's work. Only the Chief Rabbi, in his pronouncements, makes any attempt to suggest that what she is trying to do might be pleasing to God.'[6]

Judaism's concern for the poor

The obligation in Jewish law is to give 10% of one's income, which implies a process of evening up injustices in a far from ideal world.[7] The moral obligation to give 'charity' (*tzedakah*) is combined with an expectation of the poorer elements of society that they will receive it. In mediaeval and later times, that charity meant money to enable the community elders to provide for a hand-out of food on a daily basis to the destitute, and for the provision of dowries for poor girls so that they could get married (to provide two very practical examples). Haim Cohn, former Israeli Attorney General, makes the excellent point that the duty to give *tzedakah*, this 10% social justice payment, implies a collateral right on the part of the poor to receive it.[8]

This is combined with an emphasis on particular ways of giving, especially doing it such a way as to liberate the poor person from ever needing to ask again. The great Jewish teacher Maimonides listed that as the highest of his eight orders of charity, starting at giving willingly but not enough, going through giving grudgingly to giving to an unknown recipient, and so on, until the highest of them all. Giving 10% gave one no special moral virtue, no credit points. To obtain that, one had to give 20%

or more, perform physical acts oneself, acts called 'deeds of lovingkindness' (*gemilut chasadim*).

Indeed, it is those acts of lovingkindness which are the supreme demonstration of charity as Christians would understand it. The basic 10% is merely a form of social taxation, but with the freedom to give it to whom one chooses. It is acts of lovingkindness, the willingness to scrub the floor oneself, clean up the mess from an incontinent old lady, mop up the vomit, deal with the stench, which come nearer to Christian concepts of *caritas*, charity, than the morally upright, accepted command to give *tzedakah*, the 10% of one's income one can indubitably spare, and which the poor, at least on some interpretations, have a right to receive.

Human dignity and human rights

All this is well attested long before the concept of basic and fundamental human rights ever existed, such as those enshrined in the UN covenants on civil and political rights, including the rights to food and housing. The supreme dignity of humanity, which is essential to a concept of human rights, is enshrined in early biblical texts. Creation itself is in 'the image of God'. *Tzedakah*, social justice payments, are to be made to anyone, not just Jews, for need occurs irrespective of colour, class and community. All races are included, by tracing descent from Adam and then Noah. But the bulk of the Jewish law which could be described as being about social justice in the first instance is primarily concerned with the specific community of Israelites, covering such areas as slavery, sabbath observance, the rights of those pursued in blood-feuds to cities of refuge and the duty to establish fair courts of law.

However, those early commands suggest an underlying vision for this world, a sense of what the minimum is that one person must do for another. This is not only about the rights of the poor, the widowed and the orphaned, although there is always a duty to give to them, to support them. The concept of their absolute rights is much later, essentially Christian though deeply anti-establishment, since it is arguably the invention of the Puritan leveller tradition and John Locke. The established church did not like it, though the language of *Faith in the City* in the 1980s and 1990s is of rights and duties, and the trenchant criticisms of the *status quo* once made by the Puritans and the Methodists are now part of mainstream, established, Church of England thought.

That same tradition, thinking about rights and duties and criticizing the *status quo*, though no part of Jewish experience at its outset, has had a profound effect on modern Jewish thought, particularly in the United States, with its Declaration of Independence which traces rights back to the divine: 'all men are created equal, that they are endowed by their creator with certain unalienable rights, that among these are Life, Liberty and the pursuit of happiness.'

This is in itself a peculiar statement, as Judge Pollak observed:

By tracing these rights to the creator and by characterizing them as unalienable, the Declaration gave important impetus to the principle – which also had its antecedents in Locke's writings – that some individual rights exist in perpetuity apart from and above the laws periodically prescribed by particular kings and legislatures vested transiently with the power to govern.[9]

These ideas, about the sympathy for the oppressed, the need to ensure fair trials, the duty of the rich to help the poor and not oppress them, to 'open the blind eyes', to 'free the captive from his chains', and not to celebrate the rituals of religious worship without the accompanying moral and social duties that are far more important, were and are the meat of prophetic thought, the true social vision of biblical thinkers, and the antecedents of the social legislation of the rabbinic and prophetic tradition which was picked up as the most important aspect of Judaism by the leaders of Liberal Judaism at its outset in Britain in 1902 – they had already been stressed to some extent by early reformers in Germany, the USA and Britain.

The leader in this respect was the most scholarly of the founders of British Liberal Judaism, Claude Montefiore, who wrote a mass of essays and books on the subject of prophetic Judaism and on the relationship between Judaism and Christianity. It was he who summarized the role of the prophets and saw them as the key to the ethical teachings of Judaism, but linked this to a perception of what Christianity had to offer, and where the two might helpfully work together:

The moral principles which we hold highest are the very principles which underlie, or are exemplified by, the best Old Testament injunctions, maxims and aspirations . . . all the more keen, therefore, is the Old Testament on a good and holy earth, an earthly society of justice and compassion and love. And is not the best temper of our own time determined that, whatever may be in store for men after their deaths, we will seek to make this earth a better dwelling place for them during their lives? The Kingdom of God is to be realized upon earth as well as in heaven. It is worthwhile, it is right, it is desirable, to renovate and transform earth, as well as to expect and to look forward to heaven. But this renovation or transforming of earth is an Old Testament ideal.

And how is it to be achieved? Should we not, too, say by the two or three virtues of justice, compassion and lovingkindness? Are not these virtues the moving virtues of Old Testament morality? Think how they possesed the Prophets. How they informed the prophetic religion. Justice, mercy, lovingkindness: these are the prophetic ideals. Social justice and social lovingkindness: the prophets set in motion a passion for these excellences, which found expression in the Law, the Psalter and the Wisdom literature . . . the best spirits in Israel showed, I think, a genius for social morality, they set going a passion for righteousness. . . .[10]

It was that same Montefiore who also wrote:

Thus the prophets point forward on the one hand to the Law, which sought by definite enactment and discipline to help on the schooling of the holy nation, living apart and consecrated to God, and on the other to the apostle of Tarsus, who carried the universalistic idea to its final and practical conclusion.[11]

The prophetic calling

What is the message of justice and compassion and lovingkindness so embraced by the prophets and continued by the rabbis and the early Christians? Is it the critique of the *status quo*, the speaking out against the policies that have led to so much homelessness in the cities of Britain, or to constant racial prejudice, and immigration controls operated by colour rather than by need and right? Should Jews and Christians be there criticizing the selling-off of public housing stock without replacing it? Should we be opposed to a dependency culture? Are these political issues, or are they far more profound, reflecting a malaise about which the prophets had much to say?

> Woe to them that devise iniquity,
> Who design evil upon their beds.
> When morning dawns, they execute it,
> because they have the power.
> They covet fields and they seize them,
> houses and take them away,
> They defraud men of their homes
> and people of their land (Micah 2.1–2).

Or take Isaiah's cry on the same subject:

He looked for justice,
But behold violence!
For equity
But behold iniquity!
Woe to those who join house to house
and add field to field
till there is no room
and you must live alone in the midst of the land (5.7–8).

The prophets were profoundly and deliberately political. Isaiah was a court prophet: he was there to disturb the *status quo*. The difficulty comes when we are clearly associated, in a modern democracy, with one party with one distinct view. It leads, unless we are careful, to an uneasy silence, to the ability to campaign only on issues where there is little disagreement, as for instance, for Jews, on the issue of Jews in the former Soviet Union, or for Christians, the question of religious freedom in the former Soviet Union. We Jews have been brave and effective in campaigning for our fellow Jews; we are excellent at campaigning when we believe ourselves to be under attack, but we fail to campaign publicly for changes to the tax law to encourage greater giving to charity, for instance (a good non-party political issue), or about race, in which we have a direct and indirect interest, or about immigration, despite the fact that most of us are of immigrant stock from two or three generations back.

Yet Judaism, based on the prophetic tradition, with its strong *this*-life affirming thought-pattern, seeing this world, this life, as the stage on which God's plan for humanity and man's own route to salvation will be played out, prophetic Judaism with its message of justice and compassion, ought to have a clear view to give about these matters – a view of society and community that accords to some extent with the views of other groups, notably those of Christianity and Islam, but which has a unique strength.

But the difficulty for any community which is in a minority, and particularly the Jewish community in the wake of the Shoah, still reeling from shock and finding it hard to put the philosophical pieces back together again, is looking beyond itself into the wider communities in which it lives, and recognizing the paramount importance of justice and equity within the prophetic, and the Jewish, thought-pattern.

Exodus

And for the purpose of recognizing human rights-based traditions in Judaism, it is essential to look both at the prophets of the Hebrew Bible and at the Exodus story. For the Exodus story has a universalistic message as well as its particularistic one, especially as interpreted by some modern *haggadot*, the service books used for the Passover service and meal in Jewish homes each year at the *seder*, on the first (and sometimes second) nights of Passover:

> We too give thanks for Israel's liberation; we too remember what it means to be a slave. And so we pray for all who are still fettered, still denied their human rights. Let all God's children sit at this table, drink the wine of deliverance, eat the bread of freedom.[12]

That has to be set alongside prophetic injunctions that festivals are valueless if at the same time the poor are oppressed, enslaved or in chains:

> 'Your countless sacrifices, what are they to me?' says the Lord . . . 'The offer of your gifts is useless . . . New moons and Sabbath and assemblies I cannot endure. There is blood on your hands . . . Cease to do evil and learn to do right. Pursue justice and champion the oppressed, give the orphan his rights and plead the widow's cause' (Isa. 1.11–17).

The concept of justice, interpreted to some extent as charity, social justice, is intertwined with that crucial journey from slavery to freedom. In one sense the journey is taken entirely literally, but it also became spiritualized, symbolic, a justification for observing the ten commandments: 'Remember that you were slaves in the land of Egypt', and particularly the sabbath when everyone has a right to rest from labour, Jew, non-Jew, slave, free person, man, woman or animal.

A universal vision

Freedom and social justice, as in the giving of charity, are the mainstays of early Jewish thought about human rights and social justice. But they are also the central tenets in any vision of what this world, for these people, at this time, should be. The roots of the American Declaration may lie precisely in the prophetic, and particularly Isaianic, insistence on the nature of the human mission.

> 'I the Lord have called thee in righteousness, and have taken hold of thy hand, and have kept thee and set thee for a covenant of the people, for a light to the nations: to open the blind eyes, to bring out the prisoners from the dungeon, and them that sit in darkness out of the prison-house. I am the Lord, that is my name' (Isa. 42.6–8).

But what is the reason for this duty to open the blind eyes and rescue the prisoners? It is in the nature of a religious duty, a *mitzvah*, a positive commandment. These are rules to live by. And the converse of these duties to perform certain acts on behalf of others is their right to have that act done for them. Therefore the obligation to perform a certain duty, such as this general one of pursuing freedom on behalf of others, or the more particular ones of the giving of charity, imply a collateral right on the part of the recipient of these acts to receive the benefits of the efforts of others. Similarly, the emphasis on fair trials and a proper judicial system appears first in the prophetic writings as a general injunction, particularly in Isaiah's description of the ideal ruler in ch. 11: 'He will judge the poor with equity and decide justly for the lowly in the land' (v. 4). It then appears as more detailed law later on (if one assumes that the Pentateuch was composed over a period), in the laws of Leviticus 19 and 24, 'Ye shall have one manner of law' (Lev. 24.22) and Numbers, 'One law and one manner of law shall be for you and the stranger that sojourneth amongst you' (Num. 15.16). This is further elaborated in Deuteronomy, with the magnificent injunction, based on the precepts about equality so emphasized by the eighth-century prophets:

> Hear the causes between your brethren, and judge righteously between every man and his brother, and the stranger that is with him. Ye shall not respect persons in judgment, but ye shall hear the small as well as the great; ye shall not be afraid of the face of any man (1.16–17).

Deuteronomy is in fact a setting for the principle of the fundamental equality before the law. David Daube, in his essay on the rabbis and Philo on human rights,[13] suggests that judicial procedure and equality before the law with its roots in the prophets of Israel and its development in biblical and rabbinic law are the first signs of what we would genuinely understand as rights-based thinking in Jewish thought.

But although it is difficult to ascribe particular rights as later codified to prophetic thought, it is undoubtedly the case that the general principle of fairness and equity of rights to shelter, food and clothing such as the UN covenants guarantee so ineffectively, are in fact there in the prophetic thought about how human beings should treat one another.

'Cease to do evil, learn to do well, seek justice, relieve the oppressed, judge the fatherless, and plead the widow's cause' (Isa. 1.16–17). Indeed one could argue, as Heschel did,[14] that there was no distinction or dichotomy between justice and kindness in the thinking at all. Heschel quoted Niebuhr[15] as saying, in terms instantly recognizable to those who know well the wording of *Faith in the City*: 'Justice was not equal justice but a bias in favour of the poor. Justice always leaned towards mercy for the widows and the orphans.'

If one adds to this the view that human beings are accountable both for their deeds and their destiny, that this world is the main scene of individual human endeavour, and that human life is paramount, one can see how the social vision of Judaism largely shared by Christianity, but with different emphases, came into being. Within the law-based system there came to be a duty to do things for others which resulted in their having an implied collateral right to receive, be it the gleanings of the harvest or protection from oppression. That in its turn led to a fair judicial system, to due process, and equality before the law. That was true of Judaism as a whole, but it became the clarion call of early Reform Judaism with its prophetic forebears, and of the liberal, universalist tradition.

Those are standard principles in the modern world. For Jews they are emphasized by that journey from slavery to freedom which the Israelites took, from Egypt to the Promised Land, and repeated each year in the celebration of the Passover. The memory of that journey is adduced time and again in biblical texts to justify the duty of the Israelites to perform certain acts of charity and social justice for particular categories in society. 'For you know the heart of the stranger . . . for you were strangers in the land of Egypt' (Ex. 23.9). The story not only justified remembering certain groups in society, but also underpins the recognition of fundamental human rights within Jewish thought.

There is, of course, a further question as to what extent it is within the prophetic tradition to campaign for changes in the law. Is the concentration on justice and equity in the prophetic tradition sufficient to force us to campaign to achieve greater justice and equity within, say, the British legal system?[16] Should we not also campaign for changes in the law, and encourage the use of law for educational purposes, with human rights legislation as only a small part of a much larger task that lies ahead of us, though crucial to it? For with its constantly re-emphasized duty to correct oppression and to support the poor, Jewish teaching, particularly that of the prophets, makes clear both the required action and the basic underlying principles. And the very urgency of the tone of the prophets is to my mind one of the key factors in suggesting that inherent within the prophetic tradition is the desire to change the *status quo*, to act as reformers, a tradition which many Christian theologians would argue had been taken up by Jesus and his message of social reform.

There is, therefore, a strong message in the Prophets, expanded in the Gospels and taught in churches and synagogues throughout the world, that argues that the wrongs of this world are wrongs which men and women can address. They are wrongs which are ever-present in this life, and we have some responsibility, either for their existence, or for a failure to deal with them. These are the wrongs which politicians claim that they try to address, though some might say they also cause them. Within our traditions, there is no requirement to play a political role. But neither is there anything to stop us from doing so, particularly when that involvement is single-issue based, dealing with one specific social ill or concern. It may not lead us to the hustings, but it does not allow us to focus our thoughts only on the next world, and individual liberation or empowerment either.

For the state of the poor, or the disadvantaged, those oppressed by vile regimes or those oppressed by severe illness or disability, is of paramount concern in both our faiths. For Jews, the obligation is to try to even things up, to establish *tzedakah*, social justice. For Christians, that is only part of it, and there may well be, for some at least, a bias to the poor, a sense that Jesus himself was poor, and possessions were of little concern to him. But as much as concern for the poor is part of both our traditions, so too is concern for the enslaved. In modern times that has led to liberation theology, still in its infancy in Judaism, but well-developed in Christianity. But well before liberation theology, there was the tradition of prison reform, of campaigning against torture, of 'opening the blind eyes', of campaigning against slavery. That tradition is to be found in the prophets, a tradition of a love for social justice and social lovingkindness, as Claude Montefiore put it. The love became a passion in different ways in both faiths, and led to the social reforming zeal to be found amongst the leaders of both faiths in the nineteenth and parts of the twentieth century.

That passion can, and often does, unite us. That shared vision of a liberated world, so differently expressed but often so similar in its essence, can allow us to do more than hold dialogue. It can lead us into joint, shared social action, which in its turn can bring us even closer. And as we approach each other in action, the words of the prophets will be fulfilled:

> The Lord will make in this land
> For all nations
> A feast of rich foods,
> A feast of choice wines,
> Rich foods seasoned with marrow,
> Choice wines fully clarified.
> And in this land he will destroy the shroud
> That covers the face of all peoples,
> The covering that spreads over all the nations.
> He will destroy death forever.
> The Lord, my God, will wipe the tears away from all faces,
> And will put an end to the reproach of people all over the earth,
> For the Lord has spoken (Isaiah 25.6–8).

11. A Double Transformation

KENNETH CRAGG

It would be fair to describe Judaism as a text-orientated faith in human adequacy to attain the dignified life, independent of divine intervention other than that of Torah-mediation to a human community mandated and enabled to exemplify the achievement, that all may be persuaded of its feasibility. Humanity has no larger need of 'grace' other than that implicit in Torah-command and halakhic guidance. Julia Neuberger's chapter is loyally and fairly within this tradition. It stands squarely in the scriptural passion for social righteousness as the demand of divine transcendence. It is the very nobility of that conviction that it never allows itself to reconcile to things as they are, as if they could not be otherwise. Nor does it lapse into despair when its confidence is oppressed by how recalcitrant they remain. Evil matters only because the world was meant for good, the nation for God, and covenant to prove it. Yet the very urgency of Hebrew prophethood, its experience of persistent rejection and defiance, indicate how radical is its business with society.

On its own showing it is the covenanted people, religion itself, that are its chief anxiety. 'The wild grapes' are there in 'the vineyard the Lord planted'. The prophets carry in their travail the disregard of their words. God is betrayed in the company he keeps. That would be a necessary *religious* conclusion even if it were not also the burden of much thoughtful secularism in revolt against those compromises of religion which the prophets arraigned. If religions are proposing any transformation of society, they had better start with themselves. 'The Name of the Lord' does not have the social efficacy proper to it because there is so much taking of it in vain.

So, in complete concord with Julia's chapter in its focus on biblical moral vision, rooted in Hebrew prophethood, I am thrown back, for that very reason, on a much deeper sense of the recalcitrance of the human arena and, therefore, a more realist, less sanguine, perception of what transformation must entail. I find this consonant with what the prophets sought, as also with the imagery of Exodus and the redemptive dimensions of the messianic hope to which, surely, the essence of prophethood points us.

Such realism about the human situation has been a central aspect of Christian tradition, though in modern debate with Emersonian-style optimism. Reinhold Niebuhr's *The Nature and the Destiny of Man*[1] would be an obvious recent example. However sanguine we would all like to be about the amenability of society to good intentions and about the capacity of religious faith to ensure and sustain them, we have to reckon – and wrestle – with the evident non-amenability which persists through all the human story and which makes mock of all our easy expectations. There is clearly something dynamic about what is at stake in our human experience of good and evil, a veritable crisis inwardly present not only in ethical judgments in the making but in the issues they provoke in the fulfilling. We learn that there are no inclusive panaceas, no all-remedying solutions which do not become diseased themselves.

It is important to insist that this realism does not land us in despair, nor conduce to some Asian dualism or suspicion of futility. It is to be read as the very dynamic of good within the risk of human freedom, both these understood as the readiness of sovereign love to be vulnerable in the pursuit of its own divine ends, this being the corollary of any alert Judaeo-Christian doctrine of creation. It means that the price of righteousness is vigilance about itself not merely in respect of what it prescribes but of how this eventuates in the implementing. It accepts Kant's dictum that 'there is no unqualified good except a good will', but knows that 'the good will' is always qualified by the setting in which its 'goodness' has to be fulfilled – the 'setting' being the acts of volition within and the context of society around.

Almsgiving

Are not these aspects of realism present in all that Julia's chapter offers as a thesis of hope for transformation? The point about tithing, and the will to give to the poor as an obligation properly attaching to our possessing the wherewithal, is well taken. It is also fair to ask why other faiths do not do as well as Judaism in making the faithful those 'hilarious givers' whom God loves (the Greek of II Cor. 9.7). It is true that what is given away in meeting human need validates what we retain. Islam has this doctrine in the concept of *Zakat* (almsgiving), the purifying or warranting of retention by bestowal, of having by giving. Property, in other words, is only rightly private when it acknowledges public liability. All such sentiment is praiseworthy. I can also readily agree that the *right* of the poor to receive is collateral to what is obligatory on the wealthy, so that the latter are paying a debt rather than bestowing a 'charity'. Buddhism has something of the same idea in that the monk's begging bowl affords to the society around a means of self-redemption as well as a salutary reminder of the snare of acquisitiveness.

Yet other collaterals are always in attendance on these double benefactions – the collaterals of loftiness and obsequiousness, of self-congratulation and degradation. Should the right of any be subject to the whim of some? Is that truly a 'right' of the poor which can be so blatantly ignored? Will an end to the structures of poverty ever come from a pattern which only operates within them? Will not an ethic of *Tzedakah*, of *Zakat*, of almsgiving, admirable in itself and often in default anyway, suffice what righteousness demands?

Getting involved

The same theme of due realism awaits us when we pass, as Julia wisely does, to issues of political action to which the obvious inadequacies of private benevolence must take us. We are all currently committed to the virtues of Western democracy in preference to dictatorship, tyranny, oligarchy, or the philosopher-king. So far so good, every individual counts, one person one vote – prescripts for a fair society. But democracy makes great demands on personal integrity, rational honesty and genuine community – demands which are often not forthcoming. The party system necessary to democratic processes is a remedy which is itself much disease-prone. Interests and devices can manipulate elections, public relations' gimmicks distort issues and image-building beguile the unwary. Moreover, the pattern of political debate tends to debase what it has at stake by instant mutual 'rubbishing' of policies. This may work in courts of law where presumably judge and jury are capable of discerning where the truth lies in a contest which maximizes all the 'pros' and vilifies all the 'cons'. Cynics can perhaps read the political hurly-burly for what it means and utilize the process with a certain nonchalance. But cynicism is at length the mortal enemy of political institutions. Perhaps the largest service religious faiths can bring to the political scene is precisely the hope of saving it from the radical menace implicit in its own necessities, i.e. of leavening it with self-critical scrutiny, with penitence and honesty, with 'sweet reason' and humility. It needs to do this without naively thinking that the party system could operate without belligerence. Rather, its task is to temper that belligerence with constant self-scepticism for the sake of the fruits it is supposed to yield, but which it will always put in jeopardy.

The compunction faith-people feel about the 'brass tacks' of party politics belongs here, as do the exhortations to avoid them. Yet concentration on an ideal without engagement in the detail may well be evasive, and culpably so. Part of the answer must surely lie in the sustenance faith can give to the practitioners themselves, what their Jewishness or Christianness can mean to the Rifkinds or the Heffers of Westminster, or their more elevated counterparts. Incidentally, one virtue of the much maligned 'Establishment' is to affirm the status of the state as inferior to ultimate sovereignty – 'this orb set under the cross' as the Coronation Service has it – holding it accountable to ends it may not usurp. (I have found it deeply moving, and significant, to know that I am ministering Holy Communion in our village church to a one-time Leader of the House of Commons, and that he is receiving it.) The problem with 'Establishment' lies in how to symbolize the vital principle more plurally. Surely the Hebrew prophets would agree that a state free to absolutize itself is in potential blasphemy. Political Zionism is no stranger to that peril.

Those reflections only underline the will to realism with which I began and the insistence that all prescripts have to be aware of their own ambiguity, their liability to distort the good in the very act of constructing it. On this count, a Christian has to think of faith and society on two levels. The one has to do with obligation about structures of power, political, economic and social, the other with the inner integrity of the person, with motivation and the orientation of selfhood without which all fine idealism, prophetic wisdom and high principle are neutralized. These two levels interact. Neither can substitute for the other. The first must be resolute and persistent, but it will know that what it can achieve will always be relative, precarious and partial, a modicum of what a just order and a social righteousness should be. The fact that it can never attain what it ought will not deter it. Rather, the perpetual approximateness (at best) will have to be its spur and burden. For what it ultimately seeks will always elude the strategies and structures of a sin-prone world. Yet there is no absolution from the effort.

As Julia agrees, it is pointless to have an alms-bestowing 'bias to the poor' when there is a criminal bias against them in the systems of trade, the legacies of history and the imbalance of the economic hemispheres. The ills of poverty, malnutrition, famine, deprivation and exploitation are too great for private philanthropy, too massive for 'trickle-down' theories of how market forces work. They require correction by concerted state action, for which responsible religion must be strenuously pressing and, through its faithful, as far as possible, concerting, despite the huge deterrents to which such action is often party. Their doctrine of creation will be vital to action on ecological issues, their understanding of humanity crucial to the necessary vision and drive against racism, sex-exploitation, injustice, and every 'inhumanity'.

There are two incidental points here in Julia's chapter. The personal 'poverty' or asceticism on which she seems to frown may well be, in private terms, a disclaimer of the cupidity which underlies the evils 'writ large' and – far from being an evasion of the issues – itself contribute strongly to the reproach of all that violates a fair society. The Franciscan, or other, 'cult' of poverty implies no connivance with the quite different poverty which is inflicted by the way structures operate to service the very cupidity which the ascetic indicts by personally opting for wealth-abnegation. 'The pursuit of happiness' in the famous US blueprint is a dubious formula, in so far as happiness pursued may well forfeit the happiness that is a by-product of non-pursuit. In which sort of happiness is social responsibility more likely to obtain?

The individual and the communal

The other incidental point concerns the contrast between the 'individual' (or 'personal') and the communal which writers like Martin Buber and James Parkes made so central in differentiating Christianity and Judaism – surely quite outrageously (cf. Julia's contrast between Christian individualism and the Jewish sense of being in the same boat, p. 115: 'the individual route to salvation', 'well marked emphasis of Christian individualism' and 'not boring a hole in the boat because we are all in it'). The personalism of the New Testament (on which more below) is not only shot through with social responsibility and inter-human concern, but also undergirds one of the most impressive enlargements beyond old borders of human community known to history, in reconciling the Jew-Gentile distinction. Buber's own 'I-Thou' philosophy, so influential among us all, has its deep Judaic personalism, just as Christian community is unmistakeable. It is time we all had done with this false and confusing charge of contrast between us. Moreover, there is no rescue from selfishness in community contrasted with private selfhood. We may simply arrive at selfishness writ large. There are political examples on every hand in current history, and one of the internal crimes of the faiths is their incapacity, or unwillingness, to control them. What are we to think of the Christianity of Michel Aoun or the Judaism of Ariel Sharon?

The role of minorities

The church, then, like the synagogue, has to be down among the political issues *via* its elucidation (as its 'lights' allow) of what is at stake in the conceiving and applying of policies, and in heartening and sustaining those from its membership who undertake the political arena, whether on local or national level. It seems likely that in most nations – however secularized – a particular religion will properly dominate the 'spiritual' scene: Buddhism in south Asia, Hinduism in India, Islam in Pakistan and the Arab states, Judaism in Israel and, in some sense, for historical and literary reasons, Christianity in Europe. But that 'dominance' – given a libertarian aegis – need not inhibit other faiths, in a *de facto* pluralism, from playing a due part, conditional on the vitality of their people, the perceptions of their doctrine and the quality of their resilience. (Islamic Senegal had a Christian president through more than two decades of its nationhood, India has had a Muslim president, and Jakobovits can reach the House of Lords.) Much of what they can contribute may be common wisdom anyway, or unwisdom, but the majority/minority situation need not be disconcerting or embarrassing to either, at least in the West, provided that it is on the watch against the dangers which beset the uniquely American version of such pluralism.

In their robust participation in the business of political justice, social egalitarianism and the due ordering of nationhood, our faiths will thus be at a stretch to discipline their minds to honesty in diagnosis and sincerity in action. The reach of their doctrine, or their ethic, into the complexities of their task will be the surest test of what is in them.

I must pass to the other dimension of a Christian vocation in the world which I earlier distinguished from this active one that is political, social and moral, namely the acceptance of a permanent incompleteness about it. This (as I said) means no exoneration and no reprieve, but it does mean the acceptance of failure as the price of right standards of success. We must always be alert to the ills of our remedies, the questions persisting in our answers. Social welfare produces a dependency syndrome, detecting which inspires deceptive – or wilful – recourse to the praise of unbridled capitalism. Charity dispensed means indulgence absolved. Political partisanship of necessary logic warrants verbal vituperation. Image-building requires image-muddying. Sinister factors disguise themselves in acceptable manoeuvres. There is no end to the perversity that can attend on human affairs, and religions are the worst offenders precisely, because they see themselves as authorized custodians of truth. Even penitence generates self-satisfaction, and modesty connives inwardly with pride. Often a right emphasis on being and acting in *this* world reads any other world as irrelevant. Then so long as the victim is dead, we seem to say, and not merely maimed, death closes the account. Must there not be some eschatological accounting somewhere if all is not to dissolve into futility and folly? Yet can we well envisage how, or whether, it might be? Or, writing off the fallen world, do we resort with Essenes to the desert, leaving the evil to fester in its own nemesis, while we await unsullied the intervention of the heavenly rescue which owes nothing to our contribution? How perverse would we then be in turning hope into atrophy of will.

Active commitment and inner attentiveness

These are only a few of the innumerable perversities and confusions of faiths and of the world. Perhaps we should see deformation, not transformation, at the core of their meaning for the world, with all of us differently implicated. It is for this reason that Christian tradition has long insisted – at its wisest – on a double relation to the world: an active commitment to the struggle for its improvement by all the lights and means and energies we have, personal and public, *and* an ultimate concern for the inward motive-question of the self, a question which can only be personally known and faced. The prophetic, for all its nobility, may fall on deaf ears – witness its necessary repetition. How does teaching respond to the perversity that concedes its rightness and refuses its demands?

It is for this reason that Christianity has at its heart an event which, for those within, epitomizes this wrongness of mankind. It is not, in the end, a hortatory faith, nor a blithely optimistic one. It finds in the cross of Jesus that which signalizes for all time how wrong humanity can be. Others may well see this focus as unwarranted, overloaded, even deplorable. With that response there must be a long patience. Yet 'the sin of the world' was what the first (Jewish) apostles perceived in the crucifying of Jesus, a miscarriage of all that might otherwise have been best in Jewish tradition or in Roman justice. Still, they acknowledged it as 'the sin of the world'. They owed their inception as a new community of faith to the conviction that this 'sin of the world' had been taken, carried, borne, in an act of forgiveness which they came strangely to identify as the very shape of messianic meaning – the aura of that powerful concept concerning divine action to make right the world having mysteriously informed the life and ministry of Jesus that had led to the tragic climax. They came to see the event as history's 'day of atonement' – 'the place of the Name', where God had been, as 'he who there he was' (echoing Ex. 3.14). And in that confidence they wanted to embrace the world.

This understanding underlies the twin features of a Christian ethic: commitment to action in the day-to-day world, but on the ground of an inward 'conversion' or 'conforming' into full self-awareness as both needing, and finding, the grace of forgiveness and inward renewal. Of this the suffering Jesus was held to be the paradigm. Death and baptism were to be parables of each other. There was to be a living 'No' to egotism, to the self-for-itself, as the condition of a 'Yes' to the self-for-the-Lord of the self. This was its resolution of the problem of 'desire' so central to Buddhism. It meant a necessary 'undesiring' of that which made the self inherently selfish, for the sake of that desiring by which it could be a self 'in-fee-to-Christ' and so truly self-fulfilled.

It was in these terms of 'Reckon yourselves to be dead to sin but alive to God' (Rom. 6.11) that it responded to the crucial issue of the self's reading of selfhood which it believed to lie at the heart, not only of personal happiness, but of any transformation of the world. Thus it is not evasive, or mystical, or elusive, to see the personal equation as being at the heart of all else. 'O that a man might arise in me that the man I am might cease to be,' is then the condition of all social action. It has to begin, and continue, and obtain inwardly, in order to be implemented in the world at large.

It is with this that intelligent Christianity would ask other faiths to come to terms. To be sure, some Christians have been improperly obsessed about their place in it, for there are neuroses everywhere. But when traumas are surmounted, as with old John Bunyan, faith issues in a profound serenity which works calmly to the transforming of its world. Or when, as with Dag Hammarskjöld, it remains in sharp travail as to its true peace that very tension is its light to the world.

We have to conclude that there is no transforming of the world that does not begin and continue in the transforming of the self, and that the authentic transforming of the self will take it actively, politically, energetically, into whatever else is in need to be transformed. The fact that one faith finds a paradigm of how that happens in the history of a love that suffers does not mean that other faithful, anywhere elsewhere, may not come upon the same secret of joining themselves to the work of love in the world. Where they anchor that secret will be for them to say. Those who find it in the event of 'God in Christ' will think themselves responsible custodians on behalf of all. Surely that may be described as a very Judaic conviction.

12. Precarious and Necessary Prophetic Witness

ALAN RACE

If religion is to play any role in the transformation of society, then Julia Neuberger's heralding of the prophetic witness cannot be gainsaid. The modern language of human rights and social justice, so clearly consonant with, even if not directly transferable from, biblical prophetic traditions, is rightly celebrated. Without the critical principle which those traditions embody, societies easily fall prey to fatalism, despair, indulgence, barbarism or injustice. The prophetic spirit kindles a flame of hope in the midst of impending tragedy.

But there is also a precarious side to the prophetic spirit. In a world which has tasted the fruits of critical thinking, and is characterized by a high degree of complex interdependence, perhaps most problematic today is to know precisely what counts as prophetic utterance. If the prophets of biblical times offered a message of hope in the midst of social and political upheaval, the intensity of the crises of the twentieth century seem only to rob the human spirit of all creativity and hope. What message from God is contained in the Shoah, the threats of total war, the world debt crisis, or the massive plundering of the world's ecosystem? Faced with these complexities, the prophetic voice is too easily reduced to the role of making general critical remarks about the ills of society.

So my response to Julia's essay prompts me to explore the two sides of the prophetic witness: its precariousness because of the complexity of the world's affairs, and its necessity for the sake of the transformation of those affairs. I shall consider each aspect in turn, and try to demonstrate the relationship between them.

Inevitably precarious

It is generally recognized that there is no readily available recipe for translating ethical ideals into the practical application of public policies. For many Christians this creates a sense of unease, mainly because they feel that their religious faith should assume a more prominent role in the processes of decision-making than seems allowed. Certainly there are countless issues to be 'prophetic' about. Yet beyond the generalities it is a genuine puzzle to know where the distinctiveness of religious identity can make its mark, other than as a function of Christian individual preference.

In these circumstances, those wishing to boost the role of prophetic consciousness shift the focus of criticism away from specific issues (e.g. unemployment, poverty, political reform) to attitudes towards the underlying secular culture, which is the dominant force shaping the parameters of discussion and decision-making. Here critics espy a set of assumptions with hidden dangers. As Julia suggests, whether through the pressures of assimilation for Jews or through the lure of 'establishment' favour for the church, there lurks a potential degree of compromise which kills prophetic passion. One other commentator has likewise complained of the church:

> Regrettably today official statements (on social issues) generally reflect the well-balanced and sensible opinions of the average *Guardian* reader and do little to challenge the assumptions prevailing in the secular world.[1]

While well-balanced and sensible opinions contribute more to ethical debate than does thoughtlessness, if religious insight has nothing more penetrating to offer than the prevailing world-view, then prophetic witness has indeed become precarious.

It is important to admit that the secularist outlook has brought gains and losses. On the side of gain is increased insight into human activity that comes with freedom from the control of religious authorities and metaphysical schemes. One has only to reflect on the rise in the advocacy of human rights, refused recognition for so long by the church, to realize the extent of the gain. On the other hand, the loss has been the near-complete severance of ethical reflection from theological thought. The practical wrestling with secularity in making ethical judgments is the social manifestation of a deeper problem, which is how in the modern world prophetic thought and action can be grounded in theological understanding. Classical biblical prophecy was not simply the offering of a critical comment on current affairs; it was an interpretative power of discernment, pointing to the unfolding story of God's purposes within the disturbing events of world history, for judgment and renewal. Why this power of discernment has become problematic has much to do with the depth of tragedy within world history, especially during the twentieth century, and with the absorption of intellectual currents of criticism by the theologians of religious communities.

Both the practical consequences of the impact of secularity and the theological dimensions of the problem deserve further discussion, if the precariousness of the prophetic witness in the modern world is not to have the last word. Let me therefore consider each aspect of the impact of secularity in turn.

If Christians (and Jews) cease to apply critical responses to the material conditions of society, then they will indeed be surrendering their role as transformers of that society. The alternative position that the churches (and synagogues) distance themselves totally from the prevailing secular assumptions seems unrealistic, and may be an over-simplification of the actual state of affairs. Those assumptions themselves are an ambiguous mixture of good and bad. So the argument that the churches can best make their contributions to debate, recognizing the ambiguities of the prevailing assumptions without being bound by them, deserves a hearing. In its most 'establishment' form this argument rests on three pillars: first, critical ('prophetic') comment will make most impact if it is delivered from a position of living close to political leaders, and if thereby it accepts some responsibility for social cohesion in society; second, clarion calls for increased prophetic comment are apt to miss the mark in a complex society, and therefore represent only half the truth in most concrete situations; third, there remains a vital role for Christians in deepening ethical debate, by pointing to dimensions of our humanity that are not easily susceptible to political solution, such as the need for meaning beyond anxiety about the material bases of our common life.

It is worth mentioning these arguments, for they command a considerable following among church leaders and people. However, the real question of when compromise (not always a dirty word!) has transgressed the ethical limits inherent in religious identity to the degree of making prophetic witness ineffective in practice, remains uncomfortably apparent.

All three arguments are in fact highly contestable. First, how realistic is it to suppose that Christianity (in this case) functions as a force for social cohesion in a secular society, especially when the views of Christian leaders who are close to politicians and other powerful figures, can conveniently be ignored by them? Second, the notion of complexity can act as a smoke-screen for the failure to grasp simple truths at the heart of the effects of public policy, truths which stem from the patient listening to the cries of the poor and disadvantaged. Third, the bid to deepen ethical debate nearly always ends up in practice by supporting the policies of the *status quo*.

There may be no specific Christian input on particular strategies of public policy, but the strategy of 'necessary compromise' remains a luxury if it is not prepared to risk choices that run against the cultural grain.

135

On a wider canvas, circling round the precariousness of prophecy in argumentative fashion does not match the urgency of the crises facing the world. Massive ecological destruction, the world debt crisis with devastating poverty for millions, the manufacture of weapons of mass killing and arms trading wholly out of proportion to defence needs, instability in the wake of the changing political fortunes of many nations, to name but a few issues, are the larger settings within which our lives are lived. These problems are so life-threatening that it may be suicidal to ignore them any longer. It is obvious that we cannot, as a global community, continue along the lines that have led us to where we are now. Something has to change, and it requires a prophetic voice to announce it. From a global perspective, it is not too alarmist to say that we have reached a new *kairos*, a moment of major decision.

Yet at precisely the point of new awakening, the deeper theological questions about the use we make in the contemporary world of biblical texts and tradition in relation to what we believe of the activity of God in history come more forcefully into the foreground (see John's chapter). Prophecy, as I have said, is related to the discernment of the judging and liberating presence of God in history. Julia makes this clear when she combines the Hebrew prophetic traditions with the Exodus story of freedom from slavery. She does not tackle the larger questions of hermeneutics and the interpretation of ancient texts in a vastly changed and changing world (it would be the subject of another paper). But sooner or later we bump up against them.

It is worth considering this further from discussion of the language of the 'kingdom of God' in Christian discourse. From out of a line of prophetic witness (symbolized in the Gospel traditions by his connection with John the Baptizer and by the application of prophetic texts to explain his significance), Jesus announced the coming kingdom of God. He did so by speaking disturbingly in parables, by keeping company with undesirable 'tax collectors and sinners', by confronting the fixed attitudes of religious leaders, and by arousing the suspicions of the Roman authorities, leading eventually to his death. The language of the kingdom was the language of justice and righteousness, and reflected the eschatological expectation which some Jewish groups entertained of the imminent rule of God, when Israel's fortunes would be restored and the earth show forth God's glory once again.

It was recognized even at the very early stages of Christianity that while the expected kingdom did not arrive, the impact of Jesus had been such that it was religiously and theologically appropriate to interpret him as not only initiating the coming rule of God, but also in some sense embodying it. Therefore, from then on, Christians would be caught in the in-between time of what has become known as the 'now and the not yet' of the kingdom. In terms of the transformation of society this means that Christians can play their part in an overall co-operation with the will of God, as this had been glimpsed in Jesus, yet still await the consummation of what was begun two thousand years ago.

The problem today is what to make of that language of the kingdom, which was so much enmeshed with the expectations of the end of world history and the beginning of a new order. God, it seems, is not so sovereign in determining the direction of world history as has been assumed in the past. Put another way, given the urgency of the problems confronting the globe, we are aware of the extent of the responsibility that human beings bear for the future. In this light the sense of the underlying sovereignty of God, which has acted as the theological underpinning of prophetic witness, is in need of major revision.

We cannot, it seems to me, treat the language of the coming kingdom in a literal fashion. Nor can we transfer its hope simply to an other-worldly setting which ends up by privatizing faith and remains wholly vague. The sovereignty of God does not mean that the love of God will inevitably triumph, at any rate in terms that human beings could envisage (see Marcus's chapter). Under the traditional theological scheme, the role of human choice was always either to co-operate with what was coming or perish. I take it now that the sovereignty of God entails that the love of God is continually available to the world, in and through the world, no matter how we conceive of that offer coming to us. What is essential is that the model of God we construct be consonant with the sense of human freedom we have come to value. In the Jewish and Christian traditions, recognition of this freedom has always been there, only now it assumes a more radical form. Given these circumstances the prophetic voice challenges us to trust in the harshness of reality itself, paradoxically, as the very source of life and renewal.

How to combine this radical human responsibility for the future with a sense of the underlying trustworthiness of God is extremely difficult to portray. A Quaker writer, Rex Ambler, has said:

If God is viewed rather as the ultimate reality that impinges on us – in different ways in different situations – we can recognize God here in the reality of our new ultimate responsibility. We have been given a godlike power over life and death, a power to create and to destroy. We have also been given – or should I say, offered – grace to affirm life in and through the situation itself. For there is real grace in being enabled to act by the revelation of the hidden possibilities of a new order of life, where humans take responsibility for one another and their world. This hidden kingdom of God is a mystery; it is there for those who wish to see it and to respond.[2]

At the heart of the present global threats – poverty, ecological decay, political instability and military stockpiling – lies an alternative vision of global human community and interdependence, waiting to be grasped. We are required to learn again the art of trust, and the vulnerability of basic human values.

Inescapably necessary

In the midst of global crisis there is also an opportunity for glimpsing afresh the divine ground of creation. The prophetic challenge recalls us again to the roots of human dependency: will it be on the love of God or on the idols of material wealth, political oppression, and the neurotic desire for enemies?

While the complexity of the globe requires us to acknowledge the precariousness of the prophetic witness at the end of the twentieth century, its necessity nevertheless echoes across the centuries. The sense of the theological interpretation of history may have shifted in dramatic ways since the classic days of the prophets, but the prophetic witness connects us with the same basic choice: '. . . I have set before you life and death, blessing and curse; therefore choose life, that you and your descendants may live' (Deut. 30.19). Within that same choice the prophet today recalls us to the *spiritual* crisis at the heart of our material preoccupations with the idols of wealth, consumerism and military might.

Precisely how those preoccupations, and the material solutions to the threats they represent, are articulated as a matter of spiritual urgency is part of the precariousness of prophecy. That they are interpreted as manifestations of the spiritual crisis at the heart of our dilemmas is what distinguishes the prophetic voice from the ordinary critic of social affairs. For the global threats I have mentioned are not the inevitable but unwelcome by-products of good human management, on the way to a more fulfilled life for all. How we deal with the complexities of the problems and their solutions are themselves the means of renewing faith. At the limits of survival, it may even be that the moral protest against global threat has the status of a metaphysical claim, mirroring the longing of the divine ground of life itself for a fulfilled creation. This remains an act of faith, and cannot of course be proved. But it does mean that the prophetic interpretation of crisis has a new opportunity.

No movement in contemporary theology and spirituality has recovered the historical arena as the *locus* for meeting with divine creativity more forcefully than the liberation theologians. They speak from contexts where political and economic life is extremely polarized, such as in Latin America, South Africa and South-East Asia. Under these conditions, where choices have been sharpest, the prophetic witness has been a necessary resource in pointing to the spiritual crisis at the heart of the desperate inequalities within society.

Julia made passing reference to this many-sided movement, but her development of prophetic themes as a basis for the religious transformation of society is entirely in line with the liberationists' intentions and goals. The practice of *tzedakah*, as she points out, may not quite measure up as an answer to structural injustices as the liberationists view it, but the pressing of sociological analyses to flush out these 'structural sins' is one of their major contributions in the reapplication of the prophetic spirit for the twentieth century.

There is a legitimate debate about whether there should be an epistemological 'bias to the poor' in the interpretation of the biblical documents (Jewish and Christian) for our times, but the immensity of the global problems before us cries out for such an emphasis. The Jewish writer Marc Ellis reads the signs of the times when he recalls his own contemporary community to the legacy of the prophetic traditions:

The prophetic, like faith itself, ebbs and flows, waiting to be rediscovered by the people who bequeathed it to the world. The new urgency, represented by the burning children of all peoples, calls us to this rediscovery with a bewildering urgency. As much as any time in history, the world needs this witness, and at the crossroads of our own history, so do we.[3]

Ellis is also aware that much Christian talk of liberation has sounded too triumphalistic, and that in a post-Shoah world this is too unnerving for Jews. Being alert to the difficulties of traditional belief in God who guides history to its climactic conclusion in 'the kingdom', Ellis could be said to be fully aware of the precariousness of the prophetic witness. Yet he is equally sure that we cannot wait on theoretical answers to the questions of how God acts in history before we feel the weight of the prophetic challenge itself. It may not be possible to transfer theological models directly from 'Third World' settings to our own, but given the facts of global economic and political relationships, the prophetic challenge which these modes adopt cannot be ignored.

The new form of prophetic hope

I have been emphasizing throughout this chapter that both intellectual currents of theological criticism and the increased complexity/immensity of global problems have rendered the idea of prophetic witness more precarious than has been felt in the tradition. I have also suggested that similar experiences of crisis contain the seeds for the renewal of the prophetic witness, but now in a changed form. There is one further dimension of the prophetic witness which I wish to highlight, and which takes its changed form in completely new directions. This is the gathering momentum of dialogue and co-operation between the religions as a sign of global reconciliation. Again, this theme remained implicit in Julia Neuberger's essay, though the universalist vision inherent in her citation of Isa. 25.6–8 points in the same direction.

The struggles towards a new relationship between the religions is, I believe, a prophetic struggle. Building on the universalist strands within religious traditions, the dialogue between the religions is based on mutual respect, together with mutual challenge through ethical and theological exchange. It has become necessary for the prophetic vision to take this form, as only a shared vision can overcome the tragic history of inter-religious intolerance and war.

Now that the modern world has entered a critical phase when the rhetoric of the last two hundred years of the industrialized nations is no longer able to sustain a more equitable and participatory society for the future, the religions can once again make their contributions towards a new, post-modern future. If they are to earn their right to speak and be heard, they must first purge themselves of mutual suspicion, hatred and fear, and learn a new language appropriate for a new era. For this reason the prophetic hope, again, remains both precarious and necessary.

Religions do not easily surrender their suspicions of competing visions of reality. But once again the seeds of a realigned prophetic vision are contained within the dense maze of competing claims. For if the religious transformation of the world is to mean anything in global terms, then it must be based on shared ethical endeavour and theological truth. In other words, it must include the best visions from the many world religions.

There will be at least three aspects to the shared task: 1. to overcome the narrow theological exclusivism that continues to characterize the religious traditions and engender suspicion; 2. to sift the resources available in the traditions that are able to meet the new demands of, and contribute towards, growing global consciousness; 3. to find a way of bringing the traditions into a process of dialectical interaction which respects differences without shying away from honest mutual criticism and does not ignore what is ethically and intellectually intolerable. In these new circumstances the past can only be a partial guide to future destiny; the future agenda has its own legitimate claims.

Prophetic hope operates not against but from within desperate circumstances which often seem to admit of no resolution; hence the prophetic plea for a programme of intense personal and social purification. The call for religions to purge themselves of their deep prejudices against one another (this may be more a problem for the semitic than the oriental religions, but I am assuming that all have been implicated in prejudice at one time or another through history) seems to work so much against the exclusivist tendency in the grain of each of them that heeding the call will be nothing short of a major conversion in religious attitude and praxis.

There are two sides to the shared endeavour envisaged here. The first is for religious people to share at a practical level in collaborative action for change. The agenda for this is unlimited and never-ending, as progress in social pluralistic living carries no guarantee of historical durability. True, such collaboration assumes that there is a shared ethical framework which all can support. At the most general level this is not in fact hard to discover. For example, the joint declaration adopted by the World Conference on Religion and Peace meeting in Kyoto in Japan in 1970, when believers from the Baha'i, Buddhist, Confucian, Christian, Hindu, Jain, Jewish, Muslim, Shintoist, Sikh, Zoroastrian and other traditions met together, outlined a possible universal ethical basis for collaborative action:

> Meeting together to deal with the paramount theme of peace, we discovered that the things that unite us are more important than the things that divide us. We found that we have in common:
> a conviction of the fundamental unity of the human family, of the equality and dignity of all men and women;
> a sense of the sacrosanctity of the individual and his or her conscience;
> a sense of the value of the human community;
> a recognition that might is not the same as right, that human might cannot be self-sufficient and is not absolute;
> the belief that love, compassion, selflessness and the power of the mind and inner truthfulness have, in the end, more power than hatred, enmity and self-interest;
> a sense of obligation to stand on the side of the poor and oppressed against the rich and the oppressors;
> deep hope that good, in the end, will triumph.[4]

Of course, once we move away from such generalized statements to concrete projects for action, further decisions about strategy come into play, and depend on local, national and international factors. But the virtue of even this generalized statement is that it evokes what religious people have scarcely been alive to: the idea that common action for change is possible.

The other aspect of shared endeavour is theological. Ethical injunctions do not stand apart from theological beliefs, but cohere with them in complex ways. Therefore it is vital that 'theological space' be made for each other (see Tony's chapter). If this 'space' is not created, then the fissure between the ethical pursuit of the good of the other (the love of neighbour; to which we must add the good of the planet) and the theological pursuit of the ultimate truth (the love of God) will not be overcome. Initially it is not necessary to postulate some theoretical construct for dialogue between religions prior to their practical collaboration. But it is unlikely that theoretical work can be omitted entirely; even the shared agenda noted above can be approached from many different theological frameworks.

It may be that the theological frameworks are ultimately incompatible. Viewed as monolithic unchanging blocks of belief and practice, this conclusion seems unavoidable. On the other hand, given the partiality of human vision from any one perspective, other models of the relationship between the religions become possible. 'It might be better to see the different faiths,' writes Keith Ward, 'not as in radical opposition but as having a range of agreed values. There is an important sense in which differing faiths are engaged in a common pursuit of supreme value, though they conceive this in diverse ways.'[5] This both recognizes the transcendent inspiration within the religious traditions and yet leaves them open to movement in the light of dialogue and changing world conditions. It is a criss-crossing process of dynamic interaction that is being envisaged, the religions correcting and complementing one another through dialogue and exchange.

Other Christian theologians are similarly beginning to view the ethical domain as providing the central criteria by which religious traditions can be judged, both singly and comparatively. Many examples of theoretical models exist, but let me cite three possibilities. The Swiss Catholic, Hans Küng, has recently stipulated the *humanum* as the basic criterion for religious collaboration and dialogue. By this he intends the dialectic coupling of two propositions: that 'true humanity is the presupposition for true religion', and that 'true religion is the fulfilment of true humanity'.[6] The English Protestant, John Hick, has said that the religions exist as 'soteriological contexts' in which the transformation from self-centredness to Reality-centredness takes place, and that therefore the basic criterion is soteriological:

Religious traditions and their various components – beliefs, modes of experience, scriptures, rituals, disciplines, ethics and lifestyles, social rules and organizations – have greater or less value according as they promote or hinder the salvific transformation.[7]

The American Catholic, Paul Knitter, is more consciously liberationist in his approach:

> Still, by applying the criteria of liberative praxis, by asking, for example, how a particular Hindu belief or Christian ritual or Buddhist practice promotes human welfare and leads to the removal of poverty and to the promotion of liberation, we might be able to arrive at communal judgments concerning what is true or false, or what is preferable, among different religious claims or practices.[8]

While these three examples involve slightly varied overall approaches to questions of religious pluralism, they converge in their emphasis on ethics as providing the criteria for judging religious claims. Without the theological renunciation of exclusivism, the religions will remain trapped in mutual suspicion. Without the move towards shared ethical values and collaboration, the religions will have little that is transformative to offer an uncertain world, which is itself in search of a new ethic based on interdependence.

This chapter has been a meditation on the theme of the prophetic witness in the contemporary context. That witness is both precarious and necessary, for reasons I have given. But as the world struggles towards finding an ethic suitable for the coming global interdependence, the religions-in-dialogue are uniquely placed to present a vision of the divine ground of human and planetary life. The prophetic traditions, embodying the themes of spiritual renewal triggered by crisis, concern for social justice and equality under God, warnings about being misled by idolatrous behaviour, and religious aspiration as universal, have a continuing role to play.

The precariousness of the prophetic witness should not be ignored. There are false prophets, and those who shout the loudest are not necessarily the best indicators of prophetic witness. But neither should its cutting edge be blunted. 'The prophet's word is a scream in the night,' observed the great Jewish writer Abraham Heschel, '. . . while the world is at ease and asleep, the prophet feels the blast from heaven.'[9] Tragically, our world is full of other screams in the night, against which the prophet's solidarity becomes a divine sign. Would it be too much to ask of Jews and Christians that they unite around the theme of prophetic hope, so deeply embedded in both traditions, in order to exhibit more clearly that divine sign of solidarity? It may be too much, given the tragedy of Jewish-Christian relations through the centuries. But at a new cross-roads of global interdependence, the project of shared practical and theological endeavour would be a first step in a new kind of hope, both in healing the historic fissure between Jews and Christians, and also in providing a lead for other kinds of shared collaboration. After all, if the Jewish-Christian tragedy can be overcome, this really would be a sign of hope for the world.

Part Five
Reflection

13. The Third Presence: Reflections on the Dialogue

NORMAN SOLOMON

Introducing the third dialogue partner

All the reflections in this chapter are facets of one illumination.

The members of our dialogue group, as well as others who joined us from time to time, came together on the pretext of participating in a bilateral dialogue, of Jews and Christians. We were all sufficiently sophisticated to know that there could not be a dialogue between abstractions, between Judaism and Christianity, but only between individuals. We knew also that not only was none of us a perfect representative of his or her faith, but that both faiths had developed such complex and varied resources that the very concept of a perfect, 'authentic' representative was suspect.

Still, there were two sets of us, a set of Jews and a set of Christians, so the dialogue was bilateral. Or was it?

The first circumstance that might have alerted us to the presence of an invisible guest was that we were all speaking English, our common native tongue (Albert Friedlander, admittedly, was born in Germany, but it doesn't seem to affect his English, and anyway, German is the same as English for my present purpose!). Now, English is not the language in which either Judaism or Christianity was formed, and the group was sufficiently aware and expert that we scurried back to our Hebrew and Greek texts whenever some sensitive scriptural text was cited. But if we were talking and thinking English, then we were mediating our Hebrew and Greek traditions through another culture (for language is the articulation of culture). It was this shared culture that made the dialogue possible. But it did not – could not – provide a neutral medium. Rather, it was the 'third presence' in the dialogue, a presence whose profound influence (as Aristotle said of the 'music of the spheres') was so all-pervasive that it was in danger of not being noticed.

Three cultures – even three civilizations – met. A Christian civilization, a Jewish civilization, and the third civilization, in which all of us Jews and Christians live and find our identity, and which was mediated through the English language. This third was the civilization of modernity, or of enlightenment.

I will not attempt here to define 'modernity' or 'enlightenment', or to relate them to the terms 'modern critical approach' and 'secular humanism' used by John Bowden in his perceptive essay; certainly, it must not be assumed that these terms exclude 'post-modernist' and 'post-enlightenment' critiques. I fully concur with John's assessment of the challenge that these movements of the human spirit pose to traditional doctrinal formulation, whether Christian or Jewish. One type of 'modern' rationality is that which insists on submitting truth claims made by the religious, including those about the composition of texts, to the sort of tests that have been found effective in the empirical sciences and historical criticism. Another is the 'rationality' on which ethical judgments are founded,[1] the modern convictions about right and wrong which do not accord with traditional ethical teaching; liberal democracy, human rights and abolition of slavery, and equal rights for women are characteristic modern ethical imperatives, all of which have been or are opposed in traditional religious ethics. Then there are scientific discoveries about the physical world – for instance, its size in both space and time, the relativity of both, the nature of matter, the dominance of human action by brain physiology rather than by conscious acts of a disembodied will or spirit, the chemistry of reproduction and genetic variation – all findings which flatly contradict the assumptions made by the writers of the formative texts of our faiths.

Three cultures, three parties to the dialogue . . . Would it be true to say that each man and woman participating was a member of two cultures, modernity plus either Judaism or Christianity? I think not. When I identify myself as a Jew this does not mean that I inherit exclusively one tradition. My special relationship with Judaism is to do with which set of people I feel I belong with in family and historical and religious perspectives, and to a limited extent with truth-claims; it is not a delineation of the resources available to me for spiritual, intellectual or even social growth. Truth comes from many sources; my total heritage is everything now accessible to me, including creations of other religious traditions. Our starting point, far from being two teams on opposite sides of a high fence, was that of individuals each nourished by every one of three cultures, though each with a special relationship with his or her own religious tradition.

On pretending to go back to the roots

We all sought 'authenticity' by appropriating source texts, whether biblical or later. In reclaiming statements uttered by our forebears, are we genuinely turning back to the origins, or at least earlier developments, of our religions?

'Back to the origins' movements occur in all religions; both reform and reaction present themselves in this light. Karaism was 'back to the origins' in scripture (as against the 'new-fangled' and thus 'inauthentic' teachings of the rabbis); Protestantism was 'back to the origins' in scripture (as against the 'distorted' teachings of the Roman church). But Rabbanism also saw itself as 'back to the origins' (the 'authentic' rabbinic interpretation of scripture passed down from Sinai), and so did the Catholic Counter-Reformation (the 'authentic' interpretation of scripture as preserved and formulated by the church).

Going back to the origins is not the same as being at the origins. It is contrived. The origins were what they were at the time that they were, without being contrived. 'Back to the origins' is here, now, pretending to be somewhere else. This is the fatal flaw of all movements of reclamation, of all traditionalism. It aims to be somewhere that it is not and cannot be, and in the attempt loses contact with reality and truth.

A simple illustration, pertinent to both Judaism and Christianity. The Bible apparently assumes the earth is flat; it innocently adopts the best available understanding at its time of composition, and reinterprets these 'facts' for its own purposes. There is nothing forced or contrived about this. But long after Genesis was set down, when Parmenides, Plato and Aristotle – the last of these with convincing proofs[2] – had demonstrated the sphericity of the earth, when Ptolemy had compiled his Almagest with meticulous calculation of the motions of concentric heavenly spheres around a spherical earth, the assertion that the earth was flat had lost all innocence. When the fourth-century Christian Lactantius ridicules the 'false wisdom of the philosophers' that the earth is a sphere,[3] it is a contrivance, a conscious rejection of 'heathen' science – 'the virtues of the heathen were but splendid vices'. Similarly, today, when Christian and Jewish fundamentalists reject organic evolution ('Darwinism'), they are not innocent, but calculatedly defying the 'heathen' (whether 'scientists' or *goyim* – non-Jews).

In the course of our dialogue we often gingerly side-stepped situations in which we might have been tempted to criticize each other's doctrines. To some extent this was to avoid mutual annoyance, to build confidence by focusing on what we shared rather than on what divided us. Yet there was a deeper reason why none of us would have been comfortable with that sort of criticism. Precisely because, immersed in the modern world, we are not the same sort of believers as our predecessors were, we could not properly talk to and about each other in the way they did; it would just not ring true.

In earlier times, our critique of each other's doctrines arose from our own 'innocent' convictions about the world, our own naive faith. Christians have denied salvation to non-believers, including adherents of other faiths, on the grounds that Jesus said 'No one comes to the Father except through me' (John 14.6). There was nothing contrived about such Christian belief in pre-modern times, nothing in the prevailing world-view to counter it; to believers in the New Testament it seemed correct and reasonable to accept the Johannine text as irrefutable evidence as to what Jesus actually said, to interpret it as specifying the unique path to salvation, and to accept Jesus' reported words as authoritative. Yet each of those assumptions would now be questioned by scholars. Only the ignorant could be 'innocent' exclusivists on the basis of John; better informed people who continue in that vein are no longer 'innocent', but by a contrived 'act of faith' have rejected modernity.

Likewise, if I ask myself why I reject christological doctrines such as incarnation, it would be self-deception to think that this was because they contradicted this, that or the other Jewish text. In conversation I may cite a verse or rabbinic apophthegm, but this is not 'innocent'; it is a shorthand, conveniently linking my modern 'rationality' with the tradition that forms my identity: modernity has displaced text-based Judaism as my criterion of truth. I object to christology not primarily as a Jew but as a human being ('secular humanism'). Does my attitude to christology differ from that of a liberal Christian such as John Hick or his colleagues of *The Myth of God Incarnate* fame (see John's essay)? Certainly not so far as the process of 'demythologization' is concerned. The difference between us becomes apparent when we consider the later *The Myth of Christian Uniqueness* volume, edited by John Hick with Paul Knitter.[4] It lies not in the content or nature of belief, but in commitment to a system of symbols in which 'the incarnate God' has a central position. Like contributors to *The Myth of Christian Uniqueness*, I can read christology as a metaphor of deep truth; like me, they can be aware of the dangers and limitations of the metaphor. In claiming to be Christians, they commit themselves to a peculiar social use of the metaphor; it becomes a sign of community, a social bond, and the starting point of discourse about 'ultimate reality'. In not being a Christian, I am declining to use it in these ways.

What was meant to be a dialogue between Christians and Jews as Christians and Jews is again revealed as a tripartite dialogue in which the third partner is the modern world-view. Unless the third partner is recognized, an element of falsity remains in the dialogue. Traditional postures are adopted, minds do not meet.

The Quixote – the wheel that is reinvented is not the same wheel

Jorge Luis Borges tells a story of 'Pierre Menard, Author of the Quixote'[5] who, in the twentieth century, rewrites whole sections of Cervantes' classic word for word, yet without referring to the original. Menard has familiarized himself with seventeenth-century Spanish, rediscovered the Catholic faith, warred against the Moors, forgotten the subsequent history of Europe, all in order to *be* Cervantes, to *recreate* (not to copy, not to plagiarize) the original text. And Borges astonishes us: 'The text of Cervantes and that of Menard are verbally identical, but the second is almost infinitely richer!'

The papers in the present book contain original texts and ideas; but it is not always that which is novel which is richest. As we met over the years, testing each other out, seeking trust, pooling information, we re-created, in our unique context, ideas and even sentences that others had created before us (though we did not always know they had). It is the unique context which enriches the words, the same yet subtly and powerfully different from the words of the dead (dead, for this purpose, being an author whose book has left his hand, though he may remain irrelevantly alive).

Borges asks, how would the reader know whether the Quixote he was reading was that of Cervantes or that of Menard? Or his very own? For in merely reading Quixote the reader creates his own Quixote.

Bayfield reinvents al-Fayyumi

Tony Bayfield, in his opening article 'Making Theological Space', writes:

Religion is a culturally and historically moulded inheritance (p. 26).

and:

Religion for me is about meaning, about encounter and experience, about duty and the realization of goodness (p. 25).

and again:

Christ comes to the dialogue room ... Fascinating, perplexing, enlightening, puzzling, distinctive – not my God. And yet, as it were, an outpouring and an outreaching of the Ein Sof . . . whom, I believe, both Jews and Christians address (p. 27).

(Confusion here between 'my God', 'my mental image of God', 'my way to God'?) And even more strongly:

Clearly this is to acknowledge the New Testament as a book of revelation (p. 22).

I shall not now question Tony's assessment of the Christian truth claim (though I am one of the Jews he laments who thinks that 'Christianity is based on a mistake'). I shall concede that he has reached his position through reflection on the source texts of Judaism and Christianity and on his experiences of Judaism and Christianity as living faiths; he has shown himself sensitive to the common experiences that are signified in the symbols around which each faith community rallies. His conclusion is original, for it is not transcribed from anywhere, but arises as he articulates the depths of his own being.

Yet there is something very curious here, maddeningly akin to the creative achievement of Pierre Menard, author of *the* Quixote. In fact, Tony has reinvented a substantial section of the *Bustan el-Uqul* (the *Garden of Intellects*) of the twelfth-century Jewish Neoplatonist Nethanel al-Fayyumi.[6] Nethanel has 'an entirely naturalistic conception of revelation: God continually causes His goodness and His perfections to emanate towards the Universal Soul, from which the divine influx emanates eternally towards the sages who are able to receive it and, since all the peoples have the right to be saved, each nation receives from its prophet the revelation appropriate to it, in the language that it speaks'.[7] Nethanel, moreover, shows every sign of recognizing Muhammad as a prophet, and he discovers deep mysteries in the Qur'an. Tony's concept of revelation is certainly 'naturalistic': his emphasis on the social context of religion corresponds to Nethanel's idea that each nation receives an appropriate revelation in its own language; his attitude to the New Testament is not unlike that of Nethanel to the Qur'an; and his concept of Jesus as the way to God for Christians is the counterpart of Nethanel's recognition of Muhammad's prophecy.

Has Tony 'rewritten' the text of Nethanel, if in a Christian rather than an Ismaili context? Like Menard composing *the* Quixote without copying a single word from Cervantes, has Tony composed *without copying* the *Garden of Intellects*? Like Borges, we can observe with astonishment, 'The text of Nethanel and that of Tony are verbally identical, but the second is almost infinitely richer.' (A hyperbole; moreover, our texts are conceptually rather than verbally close.)

Four of the numerous ways that Tony's text is richer than that of Nethanel are:

(i)   It incorporates a broader understanding of the phenomenon of religion.
(ii) Its understanding of texts as bearers of revelations has been fine-tuned to accommodate historical criticism.
(iii) Where Nethanel conceives of static nations, languages, cultures, which are discrete vehicles of divine emanation, Tony's anthropology is plastic, sensitive to historical change.
(iv) 'An outpouring of the Ein Sof', writes Tony, as Nethanel might have done. But the context ('intertextuality') in which Tony pens that phrase introduces a range of twentieth-century psychological and phenomenological analysis of human experience not available to Nethanel.

In regenerating past metaphors our dialogue creates new meaning.

Can religious truth-claims be assessed?

I remarked above on the reluctance of dialogue participants to engage in mutual criticism or argument on doctrinal matters. We were to listen to each other, to take the other at his self-evaluation and in terms of his own self-understanding; we were engaging in dialogue, not negotiating, so we did not wish by criticism to hurt or convert the other. But we were in danger of relativizing religions to such an extent that nothing remained subject to rational judgment. Thus Tony quotes Panikkar (p. 26):

> Comparative religion . . . is not possible, because we do not have any neutral platform outside every tradition whence comparisons may be drawn.[8]

This is wrong. 'Platforms' are available, such as those of the philosopher or the anthropologist, which stand independent of the religious traditions. Indeed, the modern era arose, intellectually speaking, precisely when philosophers such as Spinoza began using reason as the criterion of religion rather than vice versa.

Talking within one faith about others

It is possible to find within the language of any one religion or denomination adequate resources to talk perceptively and without distortion about any other? Within Judaism this is done in terms of the 'seven *mitzvot* of the children of Noah'. This, together with the affirmation that 'the righteous of all nations have a share in the world to come', ensures that Judaism allows 'theological space' for other faiths. Tony and others have referred to this, whilst expressing reservations as to its adequacy today. From the Middle Ages onwards it has been normal for Jewish teachers, following Halevi and Maimonides, to affirm the value of other faiths, whilst continuing to regard the truths of their own faith as superior to those of all others and as objectively correct; and we have seen that Nethanel al-Fayyumi held that fully authentic revelations were granted to people other than Israel.

Christians have had greater difficulty than Jews or Muslims in finding 'theological space' for other faiths. Our own Christian participants desperately wanted to find such 'space', but ran up against (*a*) a desire to uphold the unique significance of the 'saving' work of Jesus Christ and (*b*) a doctrine of salvation resting on what, to non-Christians (not only Jews), is the bizarre idea that without the intervention of Jesus the world is 'damned'. The problem is sharply expressed in the text Margaret Shepherd cites from Jacques Pohier:

> . . . how does one recognize the religious value of the other religions without devaluing the unique role of Jesus Christ in the encounter between God and human beings? How does one stress the unique role of Jesus Christ in this encounter without devaluing the real religious worth of the other religions? (above p. 42)

Yet Pohier himself does not seem to grasp that it is not only the claim of the uniqueness of Jesus but the ontological claim of the unredeemed nature of the world which undermines Christian attempts to 'make room' for other faiths.

Since none of our Christians relished full-blown traditional Christian 'exclusivism', they ranged between 'inclusivism' and genuine 'pluralism'. At the time of the dialogue we were unaware that two Vatican Commissions were jointly preparing a document on Dialogue and Evangelism which explicitly (if not consistently) adopted the inclusivist position, asserting that even those who reject Christ might be 'saved':

> . . . it will be in the sincere practice of what is good in their own religious traditions and by following the dictates of their conscience that the members of other religions respond positively to God's invitation and receive salvation in Jesus Christ, even while they do not recognize or acknowledge him as their saviour.[9]

The inclusivist position is like that of traditional Judaism, which sees Christianity and Islam as 'anonymous', incomplete forms of Judaism. However, the salvation-oriented Christian cannot stop at the point where he recognizes 'mere' virtue or even revelation in another faith. 'Revelation – Yes! Salvation – No!' are Paul Knitter's graphic headings for the mainline, christocentric Protestant model (which he does not endorse) of interfaith relationships.[10]

Both the Noachide approach and the 'inclusivist' Christian approach make a specific interpretation of one religion the criterion for judgment of all. Where a global theology (Wilfred Cantwell Smith's term) is needed, they provide only a local theology. 'Theological space' has been generated, as Margaret Shepherd remarks, 'grudgingly'; no language has been formed to articulate other faiths without distortion.

The fact that the resources within each religion are insufficient for constructing a global theology does not mean that a global theology, or a non-theological approach to religions in general, is unattainable. Pluralist theologies such as those of Panikkar, Samartha and Hick are available; often, Christians achieve pluralism by compromising traditional views on the uniqueness of Christ.

Talking about faiths from 'outside'

Since F. Max Müller devised *Religionswissenschaft* as an objective, non-normative science, many 'platforms' have been constructed from which to consider religions. Some of the new disciplines are merely descriptive, others evaluative.

Psychological accounts of religion, especially reductionist ones, such as Freud's, reveal some of the self-deception that is common amongst the religious with regard to their motivation; but they leave untouched major aspects of religious attitudes and behaviour.

Attempts to use common symbolism (as Jung's 'archetypes of the unconscious') to establish similarity of religious experience across faith (doctrinal) boundaries are helpful, but leave out of each religion much that its adherents consider essential.

Sociological descriptions (Weber onwards) of the structure and dynamics of the faith community/society are useful, and explain much about the 'cumulative tradition'. However, they do not address themselves to the experiential and ontological questions which concern believers.

Much the same is true of other methods, e.g. anthropological, including structuralist, accounts of common forms of religious life, society and activities (Mircea Eliade, Claude Lévi-Strauss).

Is there a 'common essence', or an experience common to religions? Arnold Toynbee suggested that all religions share the following insights:[11]

(i) The universe is mysterious, not contained in itself or in humanity.

(ii) The meaning of the universe is found in an Absolute Reality.

(iii) This presence contains not only truth but also good; people should strive to experience it and be in harmony with it.

(iv) To achieve this harmony people must cease being self-centred.

Toynbee ignores real differences between the religions on precisely these points, and his idea of what is essential in religions differs from what adherents of the religions consider essential.

Wilfrid Cantwell Smith (he prefers 'faith' and 'cumulative tradition' to 'religion') is sounder historically. For him 'faith' is the unifying concept; it is 'what one feels and the way one lives when one encounters what Smith calls "transcendence" '.[12] History thus becomes the discipline within which religions are studied.

The problem with these approaches lies in the difficulty of coming up with any description of the transcendent ('faith') experience which is not completely vacuous and which can distinguish it from states definable (at least in principle) in non-transcendent psychological or physiological terms.

Exactly the same difficulty confronts the attempts of Husserl and others to define religious experience in phenomenological terms. Is a phenomenology of religion possible? The description of the 'phenomenon' usually demands stripping so much away from the reality that one wonders whether anything at all is left. It is rather like tightening one's grip on a handful of fine-grained sand, only to find that the tighter the grip the more sand is squeezed out. Antonio Barbosa da Silva has argued, on a phenomenological basis, that there is a common, describable, irreducible element in all mystical experience; but he acknowledges that this must be complemented by an ontology which would allow one to discriminate between conflicting truth claims.[13] At best this sort of approach can never give a satisfactory account of religion as a full cultural/historical phenomenon.

Such truth-claims as remain when the psychological and social significance of religious talk and symbols have been revealed must be tested in the light of a satisfactory epistemology.

It is undoubtedly a tough assignment to examine religions from all these perspectives (and there are others), but it is enabled by and demanded in our Enlightenment culture, and dialogue is shallow if such issues are shirked; certainly, we must not regard religion uncritically, whether our own or that of others.

Shoah, suffering and theodicy[14]

The Shoah may be historically unique, but it is far from the only occasion on which Jews have suffered terribly. Earlier occasions – the fall of Jerusalem in 586 BCE, the destruction of the Temple in 70, the expulsion from Spain in 1492 – were followed by reaffirmations and developments of the 'classical' theory of suffering as punishment for sin. Yet howls of protest greet those who advance such theology now.[15] Why?

Holocaust theologians insist that the Shoah was not only quantitatively but qualitatively different from previous suffering. It introduced a *novum* (Fackenheim), a *tremendum* (Arthur A. Cohen), which invalidates previous responses to suffering. Colin Eimer has elaborated on this.

Certainly, it is more horrible for a million to perish than for one to perish, and it is more horrible to be subjected to humiliation and killed than to be killed without humiliation. Also, some of the traditional 'answers' are harder to apply to large numbers than small; for instance, if a mere handful of righteous people suffer apparent injustice we can easily convince ourselves that despite all appearances they were not really righteous, whereas if millions suffer it becomes much less reasonable to suggest that *all* of them were really evil. But this is an effect of quantity, not of quality.

Even if the Shoah was in significant ways dissimilar from other historical events, it does not pose radically new questions for theology.[16] The questions were there all the time. The Shoah has focused our attention on them as never before, but they are the same questions. Moreover, to a surprising degree the answers given by the Holocaust theologians resemble the answers found in earlier traditional sources.[17] Even those responses, such as Rubenstein's, which demand a revision of the traditional concept of God, follow in a modern, but certainly pre-Shoah, theological trend which, in Jewish terms, is specially associated with Kaplan's 'Reconstructionism', and in general terms with the 'death of God' movement sparked off by Nietzsche.

If the Shoah does not of itself demand a new theology, and the demands for new theologies made by post-Shoah theologians do not result in anything really new, why have so many of them felt impelled to distance themselves from traditional Jewish theologies of suffering?

There are two reasons.

First, traditional theologies of suffering *never were satisfactory*. In the words of the second-century rabbi Yannai: 'It is not in our power to explain either the prosperity of the wicked or the afflictions of the righteous.'[18] Yannai's words did not stop rabbis in his own or later generations from speculating on the problem of evil. Indeed, though none of the answers is satisfactory, they may all *contribute*, if only a little, to the upholding of faith in the face of evil.

Second, traditional interpretations of suffering depend heavily for such cogency as they may have on the belief in life after death and/or the transmigration of souls. Equally, they depend upon a belief in the inerrancy of scripture and in the authenticity of its rabbinic interpretation. These beliefs have been under attack in modern times for reasons which have *nothing to do with* the Shoah, but everything to do with the 'third presence' – modernity – in our dialogue. The Shoah has provided the *coup de grâce* to lead the modernist wing of Judaism to abandon traditional theology, including theodicy. It is not a question of a new challenge posed to theology by the Shoah, but rather that the Shoah came at a time when theology was already in a greater ferment than ever before in its history, a ferment occasioned by the intellectual movements of the modern world.

It is dangerously misleading for Holocaust theologians to base their challenge to traditional beliefs on the fact of the Shoah. The serious intellectual issues of faith in the modern world thereby become submerged in a deep emotional trauma which prevents their being directly faced.[19] The agenda for Jewish theologians ought to comprise not only the broad social issues which confront theologians of all faiths in contemporary society, but also the intellectual problems which lie at the root of theistic, revelation-based faith. It would be superficial to ignore the Shoah in these contexts, but to centralize it distorts the Jewish faith.

Notwithstanding a long and continuous tradition, from the Bible onwards, of a theology of suffering, and notwithstanding a history of martyrdom second to none, suffering has not in the past been the focal point of Jewish theology. In rabbinic Judaism, certainly, the focus has consistently been God and his commandments. I submit that there is no reason for this to change even after the Shoah. As I proceed now from the theology of suffering to the theme of religion and the transformation of society I approach the true heartland of Jewish concern.

Religion and the transformation of society

Or, society and the transformation of religion? Does religion transform society or does society transform religion? I was intrigued by Claude Montefiore's phrase quoted by Julia, 'The best Old Testament injunctions, maxims and aspirations . . .' (p. 118) Here is the nub of the problem. Who determines which are the best? On what basis is the determination made? Once again, the third dialogue partner, the modern world-view, enters, for it is in the light of this that we decide, for instance, that Deuteronomy is to be followed when it calls for a just society but not when it permits slavery or calls for the smashing of idols.

Julia is irritated with Chief Rabbi Jakobovits' intervention in the *Faith in the City* debate. I was amused by the irony of a Chief Rabbi defending the 'Protestant work ethic' (he did not use the term) against the Archbishop of Canterbury.[20] Yet the fact that one finds both Jews and Christians on either side of this debate demonstrates the futility of trying to base the argument on traditional texts and values. Only at the most general level – 'we ought to help the needy' – do the texts yield unambiguous results. The Chief Rabbi and the Archbishop adopted their respective positions, as Julia does hers, not out of texts, but out of their understanding of economic realities and social dynamics. If religion transforms society in the very general sense that it calls for help for the needy (and who needs religion to do that?), society, through its evolving moral perceptions, and through secular economics and social theory, has deeply penetrated religion.

Well before 'theology of liberation', with its emphasis on praxis, was born, Richard Niebuhr worked out, in Lutheran terms, the idea of Christ as 'transforming' culture:

> The conversionist with his view of history as the present encounter with God in Christ, does not live so much in the expectation of a final ending of the world in creation and culture as in awareness of the power of the Lord to transform all things by lifting them up to himself.[21]

This sounds impressive, and accords well with traditional Jewish views on introducing holiness into the world, on 'raising' material things in the service of God. Unfortunately, it does not get beyond sounding impressive, for it does not tell us how to move from its high generalities to the determination of right behaviour in specific instances. *Halakhah*, as a system of law concerned with specifics, is more helpful. Often, however, *halakhah* simply shunts the problem on, for we do not know how to apply halakhic rules to our own situation; we know them only in a culture-bound setting. The application of halakhic rules itself involves second-order rules which depend on broad ethical principles.[22] Here again modernity intrudes itself, for the 'second-order principles', even when related to text, depend on a hermeneutic derived from the current 'moral climate'.

The significance of the dialogue

In a series of lectures first published in 1955, the analytic philosopher J. L. Austin divided 'speech acts' into three categories as follows:[23]

    (i) *Locutionary* – actual utterance of the sentence.

   (ii) *Illocutionary* – intended effect at which the speech act (not necessarily the literal meaning of the words) is directed (e.g., talk about the weather is directed not to *inform* the hearer but to put him at ease).

  (iii) *Perlocutionary* – unintended consequences of speech act (addressee becomes evasive, apologetic).

Illocutionary and perlocutionary effects can encompass social bonding, hostile or friendly intent, and so on. If, for instance, meeting an old friend, I were to say 'You look younger than ever', the *locutionary* aspect of my utterance is the actual sentence; the *illocutionary* aspect, which is not contained in the literal meaning of the words, is something like 'I want to be nice to you and make you feel good' (I am certainly not saying 'You look thirty-four rather than thirty-five'); the *perlocutionary* aspect, if any, would vary according to the circumstances, and might include such reactions as confusion as to who I really was or annoyance at some wrongly perceived intention.

So far as the papers in this book are concerned, arising as they do out of a clearly defined dialogue situation, an *illocutionary* aspect of whatever has been said and written is that it also carries the message 'Let's be friends!' Simple as this message is, it represents the most important social and political aspect of dialogue.

There is a further illocutionary aspect. Our conversations, all in 'educated' late twentieth-century English, do not just declare that we wish to be friends, but also that in some way we share a *Weltanschauung*, an attitude to the world. In this 'illocution' our third dialogue partner reappears, for our dialogue rests on the assumption of a 'modern' or 'enlightenment' world-view, a common culture to which we are in varying degrees committed.

At about the time Austin was writing, Roland Barthes[24] came under the spell of Saussure. Following Barthes, one might regard religions as consisting of sets of images and behaviour patterns which form signifying systems. Like the 'garment system',[25] the 'languages' of religion and interfaith dialogue have their sets of images and behaviour patterns, their own signifying systems. It is, however, at the level of 'second order meanings'[26] that we will find the key to deciphering our dialogue. For the Christian-

Jewish dialogue is an 'autonomous signifying system' every bit as much as the press, or the garment system, or the Tour de France cycle race, which latter Barthes brilliantly interprets as a Homeric epic.[27]

Notwithstanding Paul van Buren's model of 'walking together' on a journey, it would be an exaggeration to describe our dialogue as an Odyssey; it lacks the heroics of Odysseus or of the Tour de France. It was a little like smoking the peace pipe or burying the hatchet, but less clear-cut, less final: we have opened up a process, not completed one. It was a celebration of kinship – 'we are brothers/ sisters', 'we all have one Father' – yet it was more than that.

The knights of the round table? An Arthurian romance? Camelot = Manor House? Not bad. We rescue distressed damsels (= maligned faiths), slay dragons and monsters (= 'fundamentalists'), perform courageous deeds and right wrongs and injustices (collaborate in the transformation of society through religious values). We seek the 'holy grail' of a pluralist, moral society, in harmony with the environment. We are all (male and female) knights in shining armour prone to tarnish as we implement our goals in the real world . . .

But no! Reject all metaphors, heroics and the cloying romanticism so readily diverted to dishonorable purposes! What does it benefit to reveal some structure shared with ancient myth? The substance, not the structure of our deliberations, constitutes our message. Our message does not need to clothe itself in the deceptive garb of legend. Naked and unashamed, it proclaims:

(i) Dialogue or die. Our vulnerable world cannot survive the persistence of traditional patterns of religious conflict.

(ii) Uphold enlightenment. The openness to receive and respond to new knowledge, of other faiths and peoples as well as of nature, brings life.

(iii) Act together to bring justice into the world. Justice must no longer be 'Jewish justice' or 'Christian justice', catching votes for the faith at the expense of others, but must be 'justice' *tout simple*, to which we subscribe in the company of all who love justice, irrespective of religious faith or the lack of it.

(iv) As with justice, so with its complement, love or compassion. Love and compassion are not the jealous preserve of this faith or that, but the precious heritage of all.

That is all. Those weak enough to demand that truth be dramatized may reflect that if our dialogue was not on its own of epic proportions, it was at least a scene in the great epic of our time, the heroic drama of saving humankind from self-destruction.

Notes

Foreword

1. James D. G. Dunn, *The Partings of the Ways: Between Christianity and Judaism and their Significance for the Character of Christianity*, SCM Press 1991.
2. Ibid., 251.

Introduction I

1. Tony Bayfield, 'Heir to Two Cultures', *Common Ground* 1987.4, 8.
2. *Common Ground*, 1990.2, 15–18, 21–23.

Introduction II

1. I have told something of my personal journey in my *Time to Meet*, SCM Press 1990, 1–10, so do not need to repeat this here.
2. Memorandum of a meeting between Tony Bayfield and Marcus Braybrooke, on 13 December 1983.
3. For futher details of this debate see *The Times*, 4 May 1985 and 8 June 1985; *European Judaism* 1985.2.
4. There has been much discussion recently about prayer together. See my article in *Faith and Freedom*, Vol.45, no.134, Spring 1992, and Hans Küng, 'Prayer of the Religions in the New World Context', *Concilium* 1990/5, xi–xiii.
5. Memorandum of a meeting between Tony Bayfield and Marcus Braybrooke, on 13 December 1983.
6. See my *Children of the One God*, Vallentine Mitchell 1991, 74–99.
7. The term 'Shoah' (destruction) is used because it avoids the theological overtones of the word 'holocaust' (burnt offering) and because 'holocaust' is now used quite widely, so that the unique horror of the Shoah is obscured. See *Time to Meet* (n.1), 102ff.
8. Eugene B. Borowitz, *Contemporary Christologies: A Jewish Response*, Paulist Press 1980, 19. See also Norman Solomon, 'Jewish/Christian Dialogue. The State of the Art', *Studies in Jewish/Christian Relations* 1, Selly Oak, Birmingham 1984.
9. See my *Time to Meet* (n.1), 38f.

Dialogue with a Difference

1. Making Theological Space

1. Following John Bowden's distinction between ideology and truth in *Jesus: The Unanswered Questions*, SCM Press 1988, 16–31. See also his chapter, 51–60 below.

2. Echoing Jonathan Sacks' references to the languages of individual (faith) communities in the 1990 Reith Lectures.

3. Eugene B. Borowitz, *Contemporary Christologies: A Jewish Response*, Paulist Press, New York 1980, 187f.

4. Rosemary Ruether, 'Feminism and Jewish-Christian Dialogue', in *The Myth of Christian Uniqueness*, ed. John Hick and Paul Knitter, SCM Press 1988, 139.

5. Though it is clear that the author believes that it is his God who rules, however others name or characterize God. I discuss this 'theistic inclusivism', as Gavin D'Costa terms it, in the last section of this chapter.

6. Mal. 1.11.

7. Micah. 4.5.

8. Hosea 2.21f.

9. 'Are not you and the Ethiopians all the same to me, children of Israel? It is the Lord who speaks' (Amos 9.7).

10. Babylonian Talmud, Tractate Berachot 58a, quoted in Borowitz, *Contemporary Christologies* (n.3), 188.

11. Tosefta Sanhedrin 13.2.

12. Tanna d'Vey Eliyahu (Seder Eliyahu Rabba), beginning of ch.10. Perhaps echoing Gal. 3.28.

13. There is a full and helpful discussion of the development of Jewish attitudes to neighbouring religions and cultures in David Novak, *Jewish-Christian Dialogue*, Oxford University Press 1989.

14. See Louis Jacobs, *A Jewish Theology*, Darton, Longman and Todd 1973, 285.

15. See Jacob Katz, *Exclusiveness and Tolerance*, Clarendon Press 1961.

16. Bahya ibn Pakuda, *Duties of the Heart (Hovot Ha-Levavot)*, text and translation by M. Hyamson, 1962. Introduction, end, quoted in Jacobs, *Jewish Theology* (n.14), 286.

17. Maimonides, *Yad Ha-Hazakah*, Melachim, 9.3–4, quoted in Jacobs, ibid.

18. Emden, quoted in ibid., 286f.

19. Ruether, 'Feminism and Jewish Christian Dialogue' (n.4), 140, my emphasis.

20. Ibid., p.139.

21. Borowitz, *Contemporary Christologies* (n.3), 188.

22. It is most encouraging to note Archbishop Carey's courageous decision to break with tradition and not assume the position of Patron of the Church's Mission Among the Jews.

23. I want to acknowledge at this point that there is a vast amount of work to be done before teachings offensive to Jews are eradicated from Christianity. Reconciliation is not effected by facile smiles and superficially attempting to sweep away the past. Contemporary anti-Zionism is often a manifestation, if not of antisemitic attitudes, of a failure to accept Judaism as Judaism rather than

as a religion as Christians conceive religion ought to be. Moreover, frequent reassertions of Christian superiority and triumphalism built upon 'no one comes to the Father except through me', which regularly grace the columns of the *Church Times*, sometimes make me doubt the wisdom of my own risk-taking. Nevertheless, there is a place to negotiate and a place to do theology.

24. Keith Ward, *Divine Action*, Collins 1990, 193f.

25. Arthur A. Cohen, *The Tremendum*, Crossroad Publishing Co., New York 1981, 98.

26. Bowden, *Jesus* (n.1), 32: 'There is a good deal that we probably do know . . . the trouble is that we can rarely, if ever, be precisely sure what it is.'

27. George Steiner, 'A Kind of Survivor', in *Language and Science*, reproduced in *George Steiner, A Reader*, Penguin Books 1984 (my emphasis).

28. Discussion of the symbol of the cross also led me to a much greater valuing of Jewish texts relating to a suffering God. See also below, Harries, 107f.

29. Borowitz, *Contemporary Christologies* (n.3).

30. Which is not to say that there is such a thing as a coherent Judaeo-Christian tradition, to which scholars like Jacob Neusner object. Cf. Jacob Neusner, *Jews and Christians – The Myth of a Common Tradition*, SCM Press 1991.

31. The coincidence is thus twofold. First theological, in the God whom each faith ultimately addresses. Secondly, ethical, in the pursuit of justice and compassion, the search for love and peace, the incessant striving to release the sparks of goodness inherent in the vicissitudes of human life. Traditions, practices, modes of thinking, metaphors, symbols, paths vary but in the dialogue encounter there is more than a suspicion of a coincidence of ultimate truths.

32. Following up the quotation from Ruether, above 19.

33. Though Lawrence Hoffman, in a very perceptive essay on the subject, suggests that this is an artistic rather than a philosophical statement. See Lawrence Hoffman, 'The Creature Recreating the Creator', in *Ehad: the Many Meanings of God is One*, ed. Eugene B. Borowitz, Sh'ma, New York 1988, 35–9.

34. Ward, *Divine Action* (n.24), p.202.

35. Ibid., p.205.

36. Raimundo Panikkar, 'The Invisible Harmony: A Universal Theory of Religion or a Cosmic Confidence in Reality?', in *Towards a Universal Theology*, ed. Leonard Swidler, Orbis Books, Maryknoll 1988, 140.

37. Hick, 'The Non-Absoluteness of Christianity', in *The Myth of Christian Uniqueness* (n.4), attempts to look at whether Christianity can be shown empirically to be 'better'. He concludes: 'The conclusion to be drawn seems to be that each tradition has constituted its own unique mixture of good and evil. Each is a long-lived social reality that has gone through times of decline; and each is internally highly diverse, some of its aspects promoting human good and others damaging the human family' (30). Looking at the contributions of Judaism and Christianity to human history, that seems the only fair-minded conclusion.

38. Cf. Ward, *Divine Action* (n.24), 208. Uniqueness and superiority are not identical concepts. Gerd Theissen, in *The Shadow of the Galilean*, SCM Press

1987, manages to present a Jesus who is unique without denigrating the different emphases and preoccupations of mainstream Judaism at the time.

39. Ibid. p.210. I believe that Ward himself no longer holds this view, but it is still, sadly, all too common. See Keith Ward, *A Vision to Pursue*, SCM Press 1991.

40. Perhaps the most famous is 'Everything is known, but freedom of choice is given' (Avot, 3.15).

41. Echoing Leo Baeck's phraseology and reflecting the twin paragraphs before the *Sh'ma* in the evening liturgy.

42. Ward, *Divine Action* (n.24), 199.

43. Ex.3.13.

44. Cf. the last page of Paul Knitter, *No Other Name?*, SCM Press 1985, 231: 'Perhaps Jesus the Nazarene will stand forth (without being imposed) as the unifying symbol, the universally fulfilling and normative expression, of what God intends for all history.' Contrast this with the infinitely preferable closing paragraph of Alan Race, *Christians and Religious Pluralism*, SCM Press 1983, 148, quoting Paul Tillich: 'In the depth of every religion there is a point at which the religion itself loses its importance and that to which it points breaks through its particularity . . .' (Paul Tillich, *Christianity and the Encounter of the World Religions*, Columbia University Press, New York 1963, 97).

2. *The Geography of Theology*

1. See Peter von der Osten Sacken's survey in *Grundzüge einer Theologie im christlich-jüdischen Gespräch*, Munich 1979. This work, and other German texts cited here, may well be inaccessible to the average reader. But they are meant also as reminders that, for special historical reasons, the quest for dialogue is far advanced in Germany and deserves recognition.

2. Clemens Thoma, *Christliche Theologie des Judentums* (with an introduction by David Flusser), Aschaffenberg 1978.

3. Ibid., 268.

4. Franz Mussner, *Tractate on the Jews: The Significance of Judaism for the Christian Faith*, Fortress Press, Philadelphia 1983.

5. Ibid., 45ff.

6. Johann Baptist Metz, 'Oekumene nach Auschwitz. Zum Verhältnis von Christen und Juden in Deutschland', in Eugen Kogon, *Gott nach Auschwitz: Dimensionen des Massenmordes am jüdischen Volk*, 1979.

7. Oswald Rufeisen was born in Poland in 1922. He converted to Christianity at the age of twenty during the Shoah and entered the Carmelite order in 1945, taking the name Brother Daniel. Some years later, Brother Daniel sought to settle in Israel as a Carmelite. In 1962 he asked the Israel High Court to recognize him as a Jew under the Law of Return, which grants Jews settling in Israel automatic citizenship. The court acknowledged that, as the child of a Jewish mother, Brother Daniel was a Jew according to *halakhah* (Jewish law). However, it

refused his request, arguing that in terms of the national-historical consciousness, his conversion had erased his former Jewish status.

8. Thomas, *Christliche Theologie des Judentums* (n.2), 267f.

9. The rabbis of the Talmud derived from Genesis seven laws which all humanity should observe.

10. 1 October 1991, p. 5.

11. Elie Wiesel, *Night*, Penguin Books 1981, 76.

3. Exploring Unmapped Territory

1. Paul M. van Buren, *A Theology of the Jewish Christian Reality*, Part II, Harper and Row 1983, 327.

2. Ibid., 329.

3. Ibid., 327.

4. Ibid.

5. Jacques Pohier, *God in Fragments*, SCM Press 1985, 58.

6. Ibid.

7. Ibid., 58f.

8. Ibid., 59.

9. Pirkei Avot 2.20, 21.

10. See Paul F. Knitter, *No Other Name?*, Orbis Books and SCM Press 1985, 154, 158.

11. Ibid., 201.

12. See 166, n.44, above.

13. John Hick and Paul F. Knitter (eds.), *The Myth of Christian Uniqueness*, Orbis Books and SCM Press 1987, 195.

14. Ibid., 196f.

15. David J. Bosch, *Transforming Mission*, Orbis Books 1991, 483.

16. Ibid.

17. Ibid.

18. Rabbi Leon Klenicki, 'Toward a Process of Spiritual and Historical Healing: Understanding the Other as a Person of God' (unpublished paper presented to an international theological conference organized by the Sisters of Sion at Ammerdown, near Bath, in January 1991), 32.

19. Mary Kelly nds (ed.), *Christology and Religious Pluralism*, published by the Sisters of Sion 1990, 40.

20. Bosch, *Transforming Mission* (n.15), 485.

21. van Buren, *Theology of the Jewish Christian Reality* (n.1).

22. Cf. Vatican Commission for Religious Relations with the Jews, 'Guidelines and Suggestions for Implementing the Conciliar Declaration *Nostra Aetate* (no.4)' (1 December 1974): '. . . these links and relationships (i.e. the spiritual bonds and historical links binding the Church to Judaism) render obligatory a better mutual understanding and renewed mutual esteem. On the practical level in particular, Christians must therefore strive to acquire a better knowledge of the basic components of the religious tradition of Judaism: *they must strive to*

learn by what essential traits the Jews define themselves in the light of their own religious experience (italics mine).

23. Constitutions of the Congregation of Our Lady of Sion, No. 14, 7.

24. Paul van Buren, *A Theology of the Jewish Christian Reality*, Part III, Harper and Row 1988, 253.

25. Ibid., 103.

26. Constitutions (n.23).

27. Vatican Commission for Religious Relations with the Jews: Notes on the Correct Way to Present the Jews and Judaism in Preaching and Catechesis in the Roman Catholic Church (24 June 1985), II.10.

28. Van Buren, *Theology of the Jewish Christian Reality* III (n.24), 199.

29. Ibid., 202.

30. Ibid., 104.

31. Ibid., xviii.

32. Ibid., xix.

33. Ibid., 47.

34. Klenicki, 'Toward a Process of Spiritual and Historical Healing' (n.18), 33.

35. Martin Buber, *Two Types of Faith*, Routledge and Kegan Paul 1951, 173f.

4. Text and Tradition: Eating One's Cake and Having It

1. I felt this problem, and others related to it, so strongly that I wrote a *cri de coeur* about it entitled *Voices in the Wilderness*, SCM Press 1977. After reading it, the rabbi friend – Tony Bayfield! – with whom I exchanged confidences remarked: 'All you have to do is change priest to rabbi and church to synagogue.'

2. In particular Norman K. Gottwald, *The Tribes of Israel*, Orbis Books and SCM Press 1980.

3. The German New Testament scholar Gerd Theissen has made a particularly important contribution here. Contrast his *The First Followers of Jesus*, SCM Press 1978, with Wayne E. Meeks, *The First Urban Christians*, Yale University Press 1983, to see the great change which Christianity underwent in this respect. For the developments alluded to here see my *Jesus. The Unanswered Questions*, SCM Press and Abingdon Press 1988, Chapter 3.

4. See in particular the important three-volume series edited by E. P. Sanders, *Jewish and Christian Self-Definition*, SCM Press and Fortress Press 1980–2.

5. See e.g. Geza Vermes, *Jesus the Jew*, SCM Press ²1983, and *Jesus and the World of Judaism*, SCM Press and Fortress Press 1983; E. P. Sanders, *Jesus and Judaism*, SCM Press and Fortress Press 1984.

6. See now especially E. P. Sanders, *Jesus and Judaism*; id., *Judaism: Practice and Belief: 65 BCE – 66 CE*, SCM Press 1991.

7. See J. D. G. Dunn, *The Partings of the Ways*, SCM Press 1991.

8. See e.g. Alistair Kee, *Constantine versus Christ*, SCM Press 1982; for a particularly interesting account of some consequences of the changes for Christian belief and practice see Michael Carroll, *The Cult of the Virgin Mary. Psychological Origins*, Princeton University Press 1986.

9. See my *Jesus. The Unanswered Questions*, Chapter 5 and most recently Frances M. Young, *The Making of the Creeds*, SCM Press and Trinity Press International 1991.

10. For some provocative reflections on the formation of the Christian Bible see C. F. Evans, *Is 'Holy Scripture' Christian?*, SCM Press 1971.

11. This famous statement was made by Benjamin Jowett, in a collection of essays entitled *Essays and Reviews*, published in 1860, which proved to be one of the great theological storm-centres of the nineteenth century.

12. Gabriel Josipovici, *The Book of God*, Yale University Press 1988, 307.

13. Ernest Troeltsch, 'Historical and Dogmatic Method in Theology' (1898), in *Religion in History*, edited and translated by James Luther Adams and Walter Bense, Edinburgh 1991, 16. It is amazing – and perhaps also a symptom of the reluctance to face the issue highlighted here – that this important article has had to wait almost a century to be translated into English.

14. G. F. Woods, 'Doctrinal Criticism', in F. G. Healey (ed.), *Prospects for Theology*, Nisbet 1966, 92.

15. Maurice Wiles, *Working Papers in Doctrine*, SCM Press 1976.

16. Publication details of books mentioned in this paragraph are as follows: Maurice Wiles, *The Making of Christian Doctrine*, Cambridge University Press 1967; John Hick (ed.), *The Myth of God Incarnate*, SCM Press and Westminster Press 1977; John Hick and Paul Knitter (eds.), *The Myth of Christian Uniqueness*, Orbis Books and SCM Press 1987.

17. See Hans Küng, *Global Responsibility*, SCM Press and Crossroad Publishing Company 1991.

18. For a particularly impressive demonstration of this, in connection with the doctrine of the pre-existence of Christ, see Karl-Josef Kuschel's magisterial *Born Before All Time?* SCM Press and Crossroad Publishing Company 1992.

19. Even a conservative scholar like James D. G. Dunn, *Christology in the Making*, SCM Press [2]1989, comes to a radical conclusion here!

20. Some of these implications have been explored in G. W. H. Lampe, *God as Spirit*, Oxford University Press 1977; James P. Mackey, *The Christian Experience of God as Trinity*, SCM Press 1983.

21. I have one question in particular which I have not seen asked elsewhere: I can understand the motives behind a rewriting of history which eliminates atrocities committed in the past; what kind of a motivation lies behind a rewriting of history which apparently *creates* atrocities in the past (Joshua 1–12)?

22. For a whole set of provocative questions and suggestions, not all of which can be as easily dismissed as the scholarly guilds in Britain and America tend to suppose, see Giovanni Garbini, *History and Ideology in Ancient Israel*, SCM Press and Crossroad Publishing Company 1988.

5. *Is Historical Criticism Only a New Kind of Midrash?*

1. The full text reads: 'Rabbi Huna and Rabbi Jeremiah said in the name of Rabbi Hiyya b.Abba: It is written: "They have forsaken Me and have not kept

My Torah" (Jer.16.11). Read instead, "Would that they had forsaken Me but kept My Torah", since by occupying themselves with it, the light within it would have led them to the right way.'
2. Manchester University Press 1990.
3. Soloviev, *The Antichrist*, Christian Community Press nd, reprinted from *War and Christianity*, Constable 1915.

6. Myth and Morality

1. Dan Jacobson, *The Story of Stories*, Secker and Warburg 1983.
2. But was not the command to exterminate the Canaanites a horrifying breach of elementary morality that invalidates the Exodus myth? So many have argued. We should remember, however, that this command exists only in Deuteronomy, not in the earlier Exodus account, which requires the Israelites only to 'drive out' the Canaanites (Ex.23.28), a command consistent with a revolutionary aim to clear an area for a new start. Deuteronomy radicalizes the command because of its campaign against the reinstitution of polytheism by Manasseh. The tradition reconciles the two versions by saying that three choices were offered to the Canaanites: to become converted and join the Israelites, to vacate the land, or to die. The choice between conversion and death is similar to that offered in the holy wars against pagans by Christianity and Islam, but the third choice reflects the fact that the Israelite invasion was not a general war against idolatry everywhere, but a revolution limited to a particular area, where it was important not to revert either to the tyranny of Egypt or to the idolatry of the Canaanites themselves.
3. Michael Walzer, *Exodus and Revolution*, Basic Books, New York 1985.
4. There is thus no real parallel between Christianity and Judaism in their common situation of conflict between fundamentalist and progressive movements. While there is deep conflict on the question of the inerrancy of scripture, there is no disagreement between Orthodox and Progressive Judaism on religious philosophy since they both interpret the Exodus myth in the same way.

7. The Power of Suffering Love

1. Harry James Cargas, *Shadows of Auschwitz: A Christian Response to the Holocaust*, Crossroad Publishing Company, New York 1990, 2.
2. See my *Time to Meet*, SCM Press 1990, Part One.
3. See for example Rosemary Ruether's 'Feminism and Jewish-Christian Dialogue' in *The Myth of Christian Uniqueness*, ed. John Hick and Paul F. Knitter, Orbis Books and SCM Press 1987, 137–48, or the article by Dorothee Sölle referred to below (n.8) and Choan Seng Song's *The Compassionate God*, SCM Press 1982.
4. Paul Barber in *The Sign*, October 1990, 5.
5. The references to Tony Higton are from an article by Tony Bartlett in *The Guardian*, 10 April 1991.

6. As quoted in Alan Ecclestone, *The Night Sky of the Lord*, Darton, Longman and Todd 1980, 133.

7. See, for example, Dan Cohn-Sherbok, *Holocaust Theology*, Lamp Press 1989.

8. Dorothee Sölle, 'God's Pain and Our Pain: How Theology has to Change after Auschwitz', in *Remembering for the Future*, Pergamon Press 1988, Supplementary Volume, 453.

9. Ibid., 460–1. See also Eugene Heimler's testimony in *Night of the Mist*, that in caring for a group of children in the camps, 'I felt I was praising that Infinite power which has granted me the opportunity of playing a positive role in the inferno. I felt that I had strength only because He was present in my blood and in my senses.'

10. Ibid., 460.

11. Chung Hyun-Kyung, 'Come Holy Spirit, Renew the Whole Creation', WCC Seventh Assembly, document No. PL 3.3.

12. Hans Jonas, 'The Concept of God after Auschwitz', in *Out of the Whirlwind*, ed. A. H. Friedlander, Schocken Books, New York 1976, 475.

13. See the warning in Albert Friedlander's 'Against the Fall of Night', 1984 Waley Cohen Lecture, CCJ, passim, and Alice L. Eckardt and A. Roy Eckardt, *Long Night's Journey Into Day*, Pergamon Press 1988, passim.

14. Barbara Tuchman, *The Proud Tower*, Macmillan, New York 1966, xv.

15. G. Studdert-Kennedy, *The Hardest Part, Thoughts on Religion in War*, Hodder and Stoughton 1918, 8. See also id., *The Unutterable Beauty*, Hodder and Stoughton 1927, 3–13.

16. James Parkes, *Voyages of Discovery*, Victor Gollancz 1969, 50. See my article in *Common Ground*, Summer 1991.

17. See Emil L. Fackenheim, *The Jewish Bible after the Holocaust*, Manchester University Press 1991, 21.

18. Neill Gillman, *Sacred Fragments: Recovering Theology for the Modern Jew*, The Jewish Publication Society, Philadelphia 1990, 201.

19. Arthur A. Cohen, *The Tremendum*, Crossroad Publishing Company, New York 1988, 6–7.

20. See my article 'The Resurrection in Christian-Jewish Dialogue', *Common Ground*, 1991/1, 27–8.

21. R. H. Lightfoot, *St John's Gospel*, Oxford University Press (1956) 1960, 267.

22. Ibid, 252.

23. C. K. Barrett, *The Gospel According to St John*, SPCK 1962, 467.

24. See *Hymns Ancient and Modern* 216 and 219, and 'Majesty', a hymn by Jack Hayford.

25. Alice and Roy Eckardt, *Long Night's Journey Into Day* (n.13), 140.

26. Ibid., 139–140.

27. Paul Van Buren, quoted by John Pawlikowski, *Christ in the Light of Christian-Jewish Dialogue*, Stimulus Books, Paulist Press, Ramsey NJ 1982, 12.

28. Jurgen Moltmann, *The Church in the Power of the Spirit*, SCM Press and Harper & Row 1970, p.92.

29. See Norman Solomon, *Jewish Responses to the Holocaust*, Studies in Jewish Christian Relations No.4, 1988, 22. See also Sölle, 'God's Pain' (n.8 above).

30. W. H. Vanstone, *Love's Endeavour, Love's Expense*, Darton, Longman and Todd 1977, 51.

31. Ibid., 66.

32. Moltmann, *Church in the Power of the Spirit* (n.28), 62.

33. From a letter to the Archbishop of York, February 1944, quoted by F. A. Iremonger, *William Temple*, Oxford University Press 1948, 555.

34. Quoted by Wilfred Grenville Grey in his *Sixty Marker Buoys for a Sixtieth Birthday*, Heywood Hill 1991.

35. Cecil Day Lewis, 'Agnus Dei', from *Requiem for the Living*, Harper and Row 1964.

36. See Choan-Seng Song, *The Compassionate God*, (n.3), 249.

37. J. Austen Baker, *The Foolishness of God*, Fontana Books 1970, 395.

38. 'Jews, Christians and Muslims: The Way of Dialogue', in *The Truth Shall Make You Free. The Lambeth Conference 1988*, The Anglican Consultative Council 1989, Appendix, 299.

39. M. Gandhi, *What Jesus Means to Me*, Navajivan Publishing House, Ahmedabad, India 1959, 18.

40. See Peter D. Bishop, *A Technique for Loving*, SCM Press 1981.

41. See *World Faiths Insight*, June 1989, 27.

42. Cohen, *The Tremendum* (n.16), 98.

43. Jonas, 'Concept of God after Auschwitz' (n.12), 475.

8. *Suffering: A Point of Meeting*

1. Gen. 22.1–19.

2. Shalom Spiegel, *The Last Trial*, Jewish Publication Society of America, Philadelphia 1967, 139, 152.

3. J. H. Herz (ed.), *Authorized Daily Prayer Book*, Shapiro Vallentine 1963, 820.

4. For example, Ex. 22.20; 23.9; Lev. 19.34; Deut. 10.19 and many others.

5. Jerusalem was destroyed because: the Sabbath was profaned; people did not reprove one another of causeless hatred; there were no trustworthy people in it; people disregarded justice, etc. Shabbat 119b; Arachin 16b, etc.

6. Avrohom Wolf, *A Path Through the Ashes*, Artscroll, New York 1986.

7. Moshe Teitelbaum, *Vayoel Moshe*, New York 1959.

8. Jacob Teichtal, *Em Habanim Semecha*, Budapest 1943.

9. Based on, for example, Mishnah Ta'anit, 4.4.

10. Yosef Hayim Yerushalmi, *Zakhor*, University of Washington Press, Seattle 1982, esp. ch.2.

11. Hillel Goldberg, 'Holocaust Theology', *Tradition*, Winter 1982.

12. Norman Solomon, 'Does the Shoah Require a Radically New Jewish Theology?', in *Remembering for the Future. Papers to the Conference on the Holocaust, Oxford, July 1988*, Vol.1, 1067.

13. Yerushalmi, *Zakhor* (n.10), 48–52, quotes a striking example of how two events, 500 years apart, were linked.

14. Solomon, 'Does the Shoah Require a Radically New Jewish Theology?' (n.12), 1068.

15. Ignaz Maybaum, *The Face of God after Auschwitz*, Pollak and Van Gennep, Amsterdam 1965, 65ff.

16. Steven Katz, *Post-Holocaust Dialogues*, New York University Press 1983, 253.

17. Irving Greenberg, *Voluntary Covenant*, National Jewish Resource Centre, New York 1982.

18. Eli Wiesel, *Night*, Penguin Books 1972, 73–6.

19. Richard Rubenstein, 'The Condition of Jewish Belief', *Commentary* (New York), 42.2, August 1966. References are to the 1966 reprint by Macmillan, New York, 199.

20. Ibid., 201.

21. Emil Fackenheim, 'Jewish Values in the Post-Holocaust Future', *Judaism* 16, Summer 1967, 269–73. He refers to it as the 614th commandment (traditionally, there are 613 commandments that can be derived from the Torah).

22. Emil Fackenheim, *To Mend the World*, Schocken Books, New York 1982.

23. Berachot 29a.

24. Tony Bayfield (ed.), 'Progressive Judaism: A Collective Theological Essay', *Manna* (Sternberg Centre, London) 27, Spring 1990.

25. Greenberg, *Voluntary Covenant* (n.17), 2–13.

26. Ibid., 15–16.

27. Arthur Cohen, *The Tremendum*, Crossroad Publishing Company, New York 1981.

28. Ibid., 97.

29. Ibid., 81.

30. Ibid., 97.

31. Ibid., 98.

32. Ibid., 84.

33. *Harijan*, 26 November 1938, in M. K. Gandhi, *Non-Violent Resistance*, Schocken Books, New York 1961, 348–50.

34. Lawrence Swidler, 'The Dialogue Decalogue', in id. (ed.), *Religious Liberty and Human Rights*, Ecumenical Press, Philadelphia 1986.

35. Primo Levi, *The Drowning and the Saved*, Michael Joseph 1988, 48.

36. Dr Ellen Littmann, Lecturer in Bible at Leo Baeck College, London.

37. David Hartman, 'Suffering', in P. Mendes-Flohr and A. A. Cohen (eds.), *Contemporary Jewish Religious Thought*, Free Press, Glencoe and Macmillan, New York 1987, 946.

38. A phrase coined by Rabbi Nissenbaum in the Warsaw Ghetto in 1943. Resistance to the Nazis is a theological imperative. He contrasts *kiddush ha'hayyim* with *kiddush hashem* (literally, 'santification of the name'), the traditional rabbinic nomenclature for martyrdom.

39. Shmuel Sperber, in *Forms of Prayer*, The Reform Synagogues of Great Britain 1977, 387.

9. *Theodicy will not Go Away*

1. Austin Farrer, *Love Almighty and Ills Unlimited*, Fontana Books 1966.
2. Elie Wiesel, *Night*, Penguin Books 1987, 14.
3. R. S. Thomas, 'The Coming', *H'm*, Macmillan 1972.
4. F. Dostoevsky, *The Brothers Karamazov*, Penguin Books 1958, Vol.II, 912. I have attempted to answer Ivan Karamazov's question in, for example, *Being a Christian*, Mowbrays 1981, chapter 5.
5. Albert H. Friedlander, 'The Concept of the Suffering God in the Jewish Tradition – and its Relationship to Christian Teaching', *Manna* 23, Spring 1989.
6. Despite the great moral and spiritual appeal of the current Christian emphasis upon powerlessness, past theologians would have wanted to qualify this both in relation to God himself and to the Incarnation. For example, one of the themes of Leo the Great is: 'For that self-emptying, which he underwent for man's restoration, was the dispensation of compassion, not the loss of power . . . The invisible made his substance visible, the intemporal temporal, the impassible passible: not that power might sink into weakness, but that weakness might pass into indestructible power' (Sermon LXXII, in *Letters and Sermons of Leo the Great*, Nicene and Post-Nicene Fathers, Eerdmans, 186). Much the same language is used in letter XXVIII (the famous Tome) 3, and Sermon XXIII.
7. W. H. Vanstone, *Love's Endeavour, Love's Expense*, Darton, Longman and Todd 1977.
8. T. S. Eliot, 'East Coker', *Four Quartets*, Faber 1959, 29.
9. *Instruction on Christian Freedom and Liberation* III, 60.
10. Dan Cohn-Sherbok, *Holocaust Theology*, Marshall, Morgan and Scott 1986.
11. Richard Harries, *Christ is Risen*, Mowbrays 1987.
12. Alice and Roy Eckhardt, *Long Night's Journey into Day*, Pergamon Press 1988.
13. 'Jews, Christians and Muslims: The Way of Dialogue', in *The Truth Shall Make You Free*, The Anglican Consultative Council 1989, para 14, p.302.
14. *The Jewish Chronicle*, 4 October 1991.

10. *Jews and Christians: A Shared Social Responsibility*

1. *Faith in the City*, Church Information Office 1985.
2. J. Sacks, *Wealth and Poverty: A Jewish Response*, Social Affairs Unit 1986.
3. Salo W. Baron, *A Social and Religious History of the Jews*. Jewish Publication Society of America, Philadelphia 1958, Vol.8, 48.
4. I. Jakobovits, *From Doom to Hope*, office of the Chief Rabbi, January 1986. Quoted by Kenneth Baker in a speech on 19 February 1986.
5. Leviticus Rabba, Vayikra, IV.6.

6. *The Sunday Telegraph*, 10 January 1988.

7. This reflects the biblical law of tithes as developed in rabbinic literature. See, for example, 'Charity', *Encyclopaedia Judaica*, Vol.5, Keter, Jerusalem 1972, col.341.

8. H. Cohn, *Human Rights in Jewish Law*, Ktav, New York 1984, passim.

9. L. H. Pollak, *The Constitution and the Supreme Court*, 1968, Vol.1, 18.

10. C. G. Montefiore, 'The Old Testament and its Ethical Teaching', in *Papers for Jewish People*, 10f., quoted by E. Kessler in *An English Jew*, Vallentine, Mitchell 1989, 33f.

11. C. G. Montefiore, Hibbert lectures on *The Origin of Religion as Illustrated by the Ancient Hebrews*, Williams and Norgate 1892, 156–8.

12. Union of Liberal and Progressive Synagogues, *Haggadah*, 1981.

13. See D. Sidorsky, *Essays on Human Rights*.

14. A. J. Heschel, *The Prophets*, Harper and Row, New York 1962, 201.

15. R. Niebuhr, *Pious and Secular America*, New York 1958.

11. *A Double Transformation*

1. R. Niebuhr, *The Nature and Destiny of Man*, Nisbet 1947.

12. *Precarious and Necessary Prophetic Witness*

1. David Nicholls, 'Christianity and Politics', in R. Morgan (ed.), *The Religion of the Incarnation: Anglican Essays in Commemoration of Lux Mundi*, Bristol Classical Press 1989, 179.

2. Rex Ambler, *Global Theology*, SCM Press 1990, 38.

3. Marc Ellis, *Toward a Jewish Theology of Liberation*, Orbis 1987, 122.

4. Cited by Hans Küng, 'Towards a World Ethic of World Religions', in Hans Küng and Jürgen Moltmann (eds.), *The Ethics of World Religions and Human Rights*, Concilium 1990/2, 118f.

5. Keith Ward, *A Vision to Pursue*, SCM Press 1991, 190.

6. Hans Küng, *Global Responsibility: In Search of a New World Ethic*, SCM Press 1991, 91.

7. John Hick, *An Interpretation of Religion: Human Responses to the Transcendent*, Macmillan 1989, 300.

8. Paul Knitter, 'Toward a Liberation Theology of Religions', in John Hick and Paul Knitter (eds.), *The Myth of Christian Uniqueness*, Orbis Books and SCM Press 1988, 190.

9. A. J. Heschel, *The Prophets*, Harper and Row 1955, I, 16.

13. *The Third Presence: Reflections on the Dialogue*

1. I am well aware of Alasdair MacIntyre's critique of the 'enlightenment enterprise' of rational ethics, and have refuted it elsewhere.

2. Aristotle, *De Caelo* 2.13, p.297b–298a.

3. See Lactantius, *On the Divine Institutions*, Book 3 (*de falsa sapientia philosophorum*), ch.24, Migne, *Patrologia Latina* 6, Paris 1844, 426f. (see the notes there for a review of early Christians for and against a round earth).

4. John Hick (ed.), *The Myth of God Incarnate*, SCM Press and Westminster Press 1977; John Hick and Paul Knitter (eds.), *The Myth of Christian Uniqueness*, SCM Press and Orbis Books 1987.

5. Jorge Luis Borges, *Labyrinths*, Penguin Books 1970, 62–71.

6. The work was published with an English translation and notes by David Levine as his doctoral thesis, under the title *The Garden of Wisdom*, Columbia University Press, New York 1908, reprinted 1966, and with a Hebrew translation (*Gan ha-Sekhalim*) by J. Kaffah in 1954 in Israel, in a volume entitled *Mahashavah u-musar*. There is a convenient account in Colette Sirat, *A History of Jewish Philosophy in the Middle Ages*, Cambridge University Press 1985, 88ff.

7. Sirat, *History of Jewish Philosophy* (n.6), 92, apparently summarizing, in the latter part, pp.106–8 of Levine's translation. I am not happy with the use of 'saved'; on my reading, the key expression used by al-Fayyumi is the Qur'anic term for 'rightly guided'.

8. Contrast al-Fayyumi's, 'It is not proper to contradict those who are of another religion since their irreligion and their punishment are not our concern but that of the Praised and Exalted one' (Levine, *Garden of Wisdom*, n.6, 109). This is prudent rather than relativist.

9. *Reflections and Orientations on Interreligious Dialogue and the Proclamation of the Gospel of Jesus Christ*, Pontifical Council for Interreligious Dialogue and Congregation for the Evangelization of Peoples, Pentecost 1991, section 29. The document does not explicitly deal with Judaism, since the Vatican handles relations with Jews and Judaism through the Commission on Christian Unity.

10. Paul F. Knitter, *No Other Name?*, Orbis Books and SCM Press 1985, 98, 101.

11. Arnold Toynbee, *An Historian's Approach to Religion*, Oxford University Press, New York 1956, 262f.; discussed in Knitter, *No Other Name?* (n.10), 39.

12. Knitter, *No Other Name?* (n.10), 45.

13. Antonio Barbosa da Silva, *Can Religions be Compared?*, Theological Faculty, Uppsala University 1986, 28ff.

14. This section is a brief summary of the arguments in Norman Solomon, *Judaism and World Religion*, Macmillan and St Martin's Press, New York 1991, ch.7.

15. Orthodox theologians commonly do this, giving the lie to Colin Eimer's statement that Maybaum is 'virtually alone' in arguing that the Shoah can be fitted into existing frameworks.

16. Colin finds my distinction between historical and theological uniqueness artificial for, he says, 'theological development takes place when there are radical changes in reality'. Maybe, but I don't agree that the Shoah was a 'radical change in reality' in a sense relevant to theology, even if nothing as nasty ever happened in history. The radical changes in our perception of reality (not in 'reality' itself)

have been matters such as our increasing knowledge of the shape and history of the universe, or of the biological processes of reproduction, or of the way scriptural texts were produced; these really have driven a coach and horses through theology.

17. For instance, Fackenheim's *tikkun* (repair) concept is a refinement of a well-known kabbalistic interpretation of redemption.

18. Mishnah, *Avot* (Ethics of the Fathers) 4.19.

19. I cannot understand why Colin accuses me of wishing to 'still theological questioning' by this remark. Precisely the opposite is the case; I wish to liberate people to engage in theological questioning.

20. I have discussed this more fully in my *Judaism and World Religion* (n.14), 49f.

21. H. Richard Niebuhr, *Christ and Culture*, Harper and Brothers and Faber 1951, 195.

22. This is not a special feature of *halakhah* but an intrinsic problem of legal systems as such; the question of how cases are decided in accordance with law is a staple of books on jurisprudence. For an influential view see Ronald Dworkin, *Taking Rights Seriously*, Duckworth ²1978. Whether and to what extent 'second order principles' are themselves part of the law is debated in Jewish as well as other legal systems.

23. J. L. Austin, *How to Do Things with Words*, Clarendon Press 1955.

24. Barthes' semiotic is summed up in Roland Barthes, *Elements of Semiology*, Cape 1967.

25. Ibid., 25.

26. Ibid., 30, 89–94.

27. Roland Barthes, 'Le Tour de France comme épopée', in id., *Mythologies*, Paris 1957, 110–21.

Contributors

STUART BLANCH was for six years a navigator in the RAF. After the Second World War he read theology at Oxford and was ordained in 1949. He served in a town curacy and a country parish before returning to Oxford as Vice-Principal of Wycliffe Hall and lecturer in Old Testament. From there he went to Rochester as Residentiary Canon and Warden of the Theological College. He became Bishop of Liverpool in 1966 and Archbishop of York in 1975. On retirement in 1983 he was made a Life Peer.

TONY BAYFIELD is a rabbi. Since 1983 he has been the Director of the Sternberg Centre for Judaism, in north-west London, the largest Jewish educational and cultural centre in Europe. A past Chairman of the Assembly of Rabbis of the Reformed Synagogues of Great Britain and the Council of Reform and Liberal Rabbis, he has written a number of books in the field of Jewish education and edits the journal *Manna*.

MARCUS BRAYBROOKE is an Anglican clergyman. He has been involved in interfaith work for twenty-five years, through the World Congress of Faiths of which he is Chairman, and the Council of Christians and Jews, of which for a time he was Executive Director. He edits CCJ's journal *Common Ground* and is the author of *Time to Meet: Towards a Deeper Relationship of Jews and Christians, Children of One God: A History of CCJ*, and *Pilgrimage of Hope*, a centenary history of interfaith organizations.

ALBERT H. FRIEDLANDER is the Minister of Westminster Synagogue and Dean of Leo Baeck College. His books include *Out of the Whirlwind: Literature of the Holocaust; Leo Baeck: Teacher of Theresienstadt; Never Trust a God over Thirty; Religion on Campus; The Six Days of Destruction* (with Elie Wiesel); and most recently *A Thread of Gold*, a moving account of his return to Germany fifty years after Kristallnacht, published by SCM Press. He has lectured at many universities and written and published more than one hundred articles, many of them concerned with the Holocaust.

Contributors

MARGARET SHEPHERD, nds, is a member of the Sisters of Sion, a Roman Catholic Congregation with the special task of promoting good relations between Christians and Jews. She is a graduate of the Open University, the Leo Baeck College and King's College, London, and currently works as Education Officer for the Council of Christians and Jews.

JOHN BOWDEN has been Managing Director of SCM Press for twenty-five years. He is an Anglican clergyman, associated with two London parishes; he has translated many books of modern theology and written several himself, most recently *Jesus, The Unanswered Questions*.

JONATHAN MAGONET is Principal of Leo Baeck College. He has a medical degree in addition to rabbinic ordination and did his doctoral studies in Heidelberg on the narrative techniques in the Book of Jonah. For over twenty years he has organized an annual Jewish-Christian Bible Study Week and a Jewish-Christian-Muslim Student Conference in Germany. He is co-editor of the prayer books of the Reform Synagogues of Great Britain. His own most recent book is *A Rabbi's Bible*.

HYAM MACCOBY is Lecturer and Librarian at Leo Baeck College, London. His most recently published books are *Early Rabbinic Writings* (1988), *Judaism in the First Century* (1989), *Paul and Hellenism* (1991) and *Judas Iscariot and the Myth of Jewish Evil* (1992). His play *The Disputation* was televised in 1986.

COLIN EIMER studied geography at the London School of Economics, and after ordination at Leo Baeck College was rabbi in Paris and in Bushey, Herts. Since 1977 he has been rabbi at Southgate Reform Synagogue and he is also Director of Vocational Training at Leo Baeck College, where he teaches biblical Hebrew grammar. He has been intellectually and emotionally involved with the Shoah since his early teens.

RICHARD HARRIES has been Bishop of Oxford since 1987; before that he was Dean of King's College, London. He is Consultant to the Archbishops of Canterbury and York on Jewish/Christian relations and has been active in a number of ways in this field, including being chairman of the Interfaith Committee for the Rights of Jews, Christians and Muslims in the Soviet Union. He is author of a number of books, including *Is There a Gospel of the Rich?* (Cassell 1992), and is a regular broadcaster.

JULIA NEUBERGER is a Visiting Fellow at Harvard Medical School on a Harkness Fellowship. She is particularly interested in issues of race and religion, human rights and the prophetic mission of religious faith. She is a frequent broadcaster and has edited and written a number of books on nursing, medical, religious and feminist issues.

KENNETH CRAGG is an Anglican bishop who has combined the ecclesiastical and the academic in a sequence of ministries in Beirut, Jerusalem, Cairo, Canterbury, Cambridge, Sussex, Oxford, the USA and Nigeria. His many books include *The Christ and the Faiths, The Arab Christian* and *The Call of the Minaret*, and he has also translated Arabic works of biography and theology.

ALAN RACE is an Anglican priest and Director of Studies at the Southwark Ordination Course. His interest in interfaith dialogue stems from time spent as a student in multifaith Bradford and through academic work in the Christian theology of religions. He has written *Christians and Religious Pluralism*.

NORMAN SOLOMON is founder Director of the Centre for the Study of Judaism and Jewish-Christian Relations, Selly Oak Colleges, Birmingham and visiting lecturer to the Oxford Centre for Postgraduate Hebrew Studies. From 1961 to 1987 he served as rabbi to Orthodox congregations in Manchester, Liverpool and London.

Other members of the Manor House Group for part of its life.

Peter Dewey
John Goldingay
Anthony Harvey
Ursula King
Fred Morgan
Anthony Phillips
Michael Porteus
Jim Richardson
Jeremy Rosen
Ben Segal
Alexandra Wright